W9-BMO-726

S_{ONNETS}

_{FOR} S_{INNERS}

Everything One Needs to Know About Illicit Love

49 epiphanic sonnets selected and illumined by

JOHN WAREHAM

SONNETS FOR SINNERS
Everything One Needs to Know About Illicit Love

1st Edition, Valentine's Day 2010

Welcome Rain Publishers LLC

New York

ISBN 10: 1-56649-959-3
ISBN 12: 978-1-56649-959-0

Printed by Maple Vail Group in Philadelphia, U.S.A
Jacket and book design by John Wareham
Body text: Goudy Old Style

For Yvonne Jean,
my beautiful, insightful mother,
but for whose sinning
I'd have not been born.

═══════════════════

I never was attached to that great sect,
Whose doctrine is, that each one should select
Out of the crowd a mistress or a friend,
And all the rest, though fair and wise, commend
To cold oblivion, though it is in the code
Of modern morals....

Percy Bysshe Shelley

═══════════════════

SONNETS
FOR SINNERS

Everything One Needs to
Know About Illicit Love

Contents

* The poet's actual words and lines—generously provided in public domain utterances, interviews, or emails—were faithfully tinkered into sonnet form, by wordsmith John Wareham.

*It is better to be unfaithful
than to be faithful
without wanting to be.*
Brigitte Bardot

*The torture of a bad conscience
is the hell of a living soul.*
John Calvin

A Lover's Guide to Sinning

An Overture to the Journey of Illicit Love

Lust gratifies its flames in the chambers of the sacristans more often than in the houses of ill-fame.
Marcus Minucius Felix

WHEN IT CAME TO SINS OF THE FLESH, what struck me most was the tight grip such transgressions held on the hearts of the nuns. I was only six years old at the time, but precocious. Noting what looked like a touch of envy on the part of these supposedly saintly creatures, I figured sinners might just be having a good time, better than me, anyway.

At age seven, I checked the dictionary definitions of sin, which boiled down to *willful violations of moral principles,* and *ardent, sensuous, longings, desires, and lusts.*

I knew what that meant.

I loved to study Buck Rogers cartoons, and my eyes would hover, ardently and longingly, over the cleavages of the hot young space trekkers who shared his adventures. Looking back, I'm surprised my lusty desires didn't melt their ever-scanty garments right off the page.

And, yes, let me confess it; even at that tender age, I lusted after a couple of the innocent young lassies in my class. On the saintly side, I balked when one of them offered to share an "I'll show you mine if you'll show me yours" moment. Looking back, however, I fret that I may have demurred out of mere cowardice.

I remember the bright day when my eye fell to number eight on the list of Ten Commandments listed in my catechism book, a thick tome dense with type.

"What's adultery, Sister," I asked.

She peered into my green eyes, the better to fathom my black heart. "Having two wives," she responded, dryly.

My parents were breaking up and my father was "seeing someone," so I wondered why that kind of thing would win a coveted spot on the all-time top-ten list.

Given infidelity's popularity, I still wonder today. After all, in an age of birth control within a financially independent citizenry, shouldn't it be okay to love and hold whomever one pleases?

But we're getting ahead of ourselves. The wisdom of veering when illicit love seems to beckon is a subject that sonnets thoroughly examine, as we'll soon see.

At age eight, I was shunted to the Marist Brothers all-boy school, a seminary whose faculty, perhaps because older students were entering puberty, seemed even more obsessed with the notion of lust.

I was never an altar boy, so I never got "inappropriately touched."

Unless you count whippings with a cane.

These humorless Irish refugees, an unhappy band of sadists, surely, seemed to get off on that. So much so that I decided to get out of Dodge (or dodge out of God).

Many days over many weeks, I simply failed to show up for classes. Instead, funded by coins purloined from corner store cash registers, I played the pinball machines in the downtown "fun parlor."

After failing to appear for an entire week, however, my father got a call to confirm my excuses.

That night, he took to my bare flesh with an ironing cord, causing me to empty my bladder as he crisscrossed my naked butt and back with raw, bloody bruises.

Next day he chauffeured me to school, and dropped me at the gate. I pretended to scamper inside, but instead waited for his car to disappear. Then I strutted back into the street and headed downtown.

That was my last day as a Roman Catholic.

They could beat me black and blue if they wanted, but there was no way in hell I would reenter that wretched Academy of Perpetual Guilt and Sin.

Getting enrolled at the local state school was like entering a sunlit garden after escaping a dark dungeon.

The was no turgid catechism to be learned by rote. No guilt, no sin, and no whippings, either. Just reading, writing, arithmetic—and getting along.

I later attempted to treat my lingering psychic wounds by learning enough to make sense of the world, and, perhaps in an act of perverse religiosity, to apprehend the hearts and minds of sinners—which is how I came to be interested in sonnets.

First, though, let me share some religious tenets about sinning that also, as we'll see, feature in sonnets:

- The morality of behavior flows from the moral state of the heart.

- A disposition to sin, or a habit of the soul that leads to a sinful act, is also sin (and so is a lusty desire).

- The soul that sins is always conscious that the sin is intrinsically vile, justly deserves punishment, and inevitably calls down the righteous wrath of God.

- Sinners can be saved by repentance, remorse, and atonement (and, if necessary, a spiritual adviser can act as an emissary between the sinner and God).

- Unrepentant sinners become depraved and will be punished in the afterlife.

Maybe so, but, undeterred by any of the above, Irish poet Thomas Moore tempted his lover, thus:

> If wishing damns us, you and I
> Are damned to all our heart's content;
> Come then, at least we may enjoy
> Some pleasure for our punishment!

Atheists might not feel any need to forgive the wickedly seductive Mr. Moore. They believe that moral codes are based on human nature and social customs, so they never say "sin"—just "wrong" or "unethical."

But, if they don't like the *concept* of sin, atheists still tend to cast a captious eye on those who offend their favored moral codes. And their decrees often include a means to calibrate the seriousness of an offence and inflict apt punishment.

My own take is that illicit lovers fall into the *Triangle of Compromise,* the three sides of which are *need, opportunity,* and *excuse.* The need, mostly neurotic, is for love missing from childhood and unmet—and perhaps unmeetable—in marriage. Opportunity typically unfolds in the presence of a kindred spirit seeking to treat a similar ache. The excuse typically plays out in the sonnets, but let's first consider the rationales of three notable upcoming characters.

- Former United States president Bill Clinton, wagged his finger and declaimed, *I never had sexual relations with that woman.* This was a neat blend of legal sophistry and flat-out denial, the key phrase *sexual relations*, being defined by *Webster's* as sexual intercourse—a delight in this case apparently forsaken. But, Bill, why ever not?

- Charles Windsor excused himself by claiming that only after his marriage became irretrievable did he take a mistress—thereby royally overlooking that he tupped that lady on his wedding eve and kept her in his life ever after. Oh, Charles, *puh-lese!*

- Governor Mark Sanford, his voice breaking, explained that he, uh, fell in love. Oh, *Mark!*

But yes, of course, *love.* Might true love excuse everything? Might it absolve every sinner who can honestly claim to have fallen under its spell?

For answers we turn to the sonnets of sinners. It is astonishing how so much passion and perception can be distilled into a drama that unfolds in fourteen lines—especially since each line must carry ten syllables (mostly), and conform to a neat rhyming pattern.

So here we go then on our journey through the clandestine passageways of desire, lust, and longing.

With, luck, epiphany will follow.

Redemption, even, maybe—who's to say?

Attractions

So heavy is the chain of wedlock,
that it takes two to carry it—sometimes three.
Alexander Dumas

LOVE IS SURELY A DEVIL'S PLAYGROUND, the maddest of affairs being sired by illusion out of need—with, all too often, the Devil making the delivery.

Perhaps that's why, in the moment of attraction, sinners sense that they're about to enter an uncontrollable fire. Christopher Marlowe captures the madness of that problematic moment in his line, *Whoever loved that loved not at first sight?*

Right!—for if Marlowe is correct, the sweet object of our desire is likely to be, one way or another, off limits. It's why levelheaded psychologists agree: *the partner we love rarely satisfies all our needs, so we deceive that ally, and ourselves, with a lover whom we do not love.*

Or, as cynics might say, we search for love until one day, unluckily, we find it. Inevitably the bewitching new best friend appears to have been placed upon our path by divine providence; a paramour we sense, or so it seems, that we must have loved, ever so intensely, in a past life.

That life is not this one, alas, but the allure is irresistible. And dangerous.

For love begins with an image, but proceeds with a sensation—the thrilling, addictive tingle of lust.

Marlowe's Kaleidoscope

I was perfectly content and riding

along in a cheerfully appealing

ambrosial lane, with no thought of swerving

until angels or devils came calling.

A light bathed your silhouette as you

turned. Then you beamed me a smile in the night!

My heart took a turn, my world turned askew

—*Whoever loved that loved not at first sight?*

Ah, yes! Marlowe's fateful kaleidoscope—

jumping jack colors danced a bright gavotte,

silence sprang with a heart-stopping lope,

my soul fell entwined in true-love knot.

It is madness, my sweet, and I'm utterly lost,

I need the fever, no matter the cost

Chandler Haste

POETS CONFIRM WHAT CYNICAL SHRINKS SAY: there's one person we're destined to love, and if we ever meet that paramour, we're done for. There's a good reason for the skepticism: we fall in love out of need, and, by definition, it is a neurotic want of which we are unconscious.

The hidden privation often springs from the absence of love in childhood. But not always. Existentialists say we need love to ease the innate loneliness of life; and that the craving to be admired for the self we imagine ourselves to be is universal.

And, alas, seldom fulfilled.

So, some enchanted evening, as we absentmindedly search for love, our eyes lock onto those of a kindred spirit engaged in the selfsame search.

That, anyway, seems to be the drama in this sonnet, which highlights Christopher Marlowe's insight into the instantly arresting power of love.

Chandler Haste's colloquial style and detached irony might be characterized as flimsy, but his work provides a happy counterpoint to darker sonneteers.

In the first line, one doubts that the poet was *perfectly content*. In the third quatrain, skeptics might wonder whether he became entwined in *a truelove knot* or merely wished to knot in naked lust.

The avowal of being *utterly lost* doesn't ring entirely true, either—more like a good excuse for jumping into the deep end of a bubbling love pool.

Great fun, yes!

But, oh, what about tomorrow?

Lust

The expense of spirit in a waste of shame

Is lust in action, and till action, lust

Is perjur'd, murd'rous, bloody, full of blame,

Savage, extreme, rude, cruel, not to trust,

Enjoy'd no sooner but despised straight;

Past reason hunted, and no sooner had,

Past reason hated as a swallowed bait

On purpose laid to make the taker mad:

Mad in pursuit, and in possession so,

Had, having, and in quest to have, extreme,

A bliss in proof, and prov'd, a very woe

Before, a joy propos'd, behind, a dream.

>   All this the world well knows, yet none knows well

>   To shun the heaven that leads men to this hell.

William Shakespeare (129)

L OVE LEADS THE HEART ASTRAY, BUT LUST
enters below the belt and takes command of absolutely
everything. So says this impassioned, multilayered sonnet,
which critics hail as among Shakespeare's finest.

In the opening lines, note the subtle pun on the words
waste and *action*, conjuring the image of the lusty waist that
drives mere mortals mad and leads them astray.

To begin with, says the poet, sinners bypass rationality—
past reason hunted—then, the moment the lusty act is completed
they unreasonably despise themselves—*past reason hated*—for
succumbing to *a swallowed bait on purpose laid to make the taker
mad*. The devil made me do it!

To follow the course of lust is to experience orgasmic
delight—*a bliss in proof*—but then to awake to find oneself in
the middle of a living nightmare.

The final couplet is especially intriguing. On one level,
the Bard offers up a calm, wise, politically correct observation.
On another plane, however, one seldom taught to young
students, the bawdiness is breathtaking.

In Elizabethan times the words *well* and *heaven* were
both slang for *vagina*. Also, *putting the angel into heaven*, was
a sly euphemism for the act of love. So, here, subliminally,
the poet is saying that the world knows the perils of entering
that tempting *well*, but nonetheless fails to shun the heaven
that leads men to this hell. And, here, yet another code word,
hell, means fiery pox.

But a nod is as good as a wink to a blind stallion.

Rubicons

Should I o'er leap the tempting Rubicon
—or sojourn blithely in a sheltered bay?
Shall I play Leda to his sleek Black Swan
—or should I never dine on that buffet?
I do not vault unseemly or in haste
but dawdle with the element of choice;
mulling, musing, I knit my brow and lace
my doubt into a prayer—and hear a voice:

> *"Leap to the top of the uppermost spire,*
>
> *fly to a place where the spirit is free,*
>
> *heed the sweet music of life's luting lyre,*
>
> *unlock all doors with an undaunting key."*

So, courage then, and chance the daring ride!
Be not fainthearted, says my inner guide.

Elan Haverford

IF TO LUST WITHIN THE MIND IS A SIN, as pious preachers claim, then this poet is on the road to hell. But a moment of choice separates an impulse from an act, surely, and in that instant we can save or lose ourselves. Or maybe discover what we're made of.

The male and his member are quickly aroused, however, and notoriously more prone to succumb to instant animal lust than women, for whom the stakes—emotionally, physically, and socially—are typically greater.

So, in this sonnet, the poet ponders not just a liaison, but the course of her life. On one level sweet and innocent, but on another worldly and sexually charged, the poem showcases Elan Haverford's sensitivity to language and easy command of the sonnet form.

Not entirely hypnotized by "Marlowe's Kaleidoscope," the apparently virginal poet ponders whether to entertain a liaison with an off-limits suitor. The sinning intent of the meeting is signaled with the allusion of the poet as *Leda* and the love object as a *sleek Black Swan*.

After questioning and prayer, intuition offers a sexually laden response. She will *dine on that buffet*, a sly reference to oral sex, then she will *chance the daring ride*, presumably with a *leap to the top of the uppermost spire*, at which point, so positioned, *an undaunting key* will *unlock all doors*.

Haverford sprinkles her sonnets with telltale Elizabethan words and phrases; *vault unseemly, knit my brow, lace my doubt*. In this sonnet she also perceptively puns the character of her Black Swan as *life's luting lyre*.

But sinners have to be liars, of course.

Tiger Balm

You want a partner to witness your life;

a someone I never found, not even

at home—yet, suddenly, you're touching sides

of me I never knew; why didn't we find

each other years ago? It's brutal that

you can't always be with me. I want you

next to me, on me—I need to gaze at

you. Yet do I truly know who you are?

Will I just be fifth on your list? One more

person who just happens to be famous?

Well, my brain says yes, but my heart says no.

I hate feeling so weak, I'm tougher than this.

Get it together and get on the flight;

we can have make-up sex after we fight.

Tiger Woods

JOHN WAREHAM

TIGER, TIGER, TEXTING BRIGHT, IN THE FORESTS of the night, let's think about these lines to the babe you hope might fill the void within the sinews of your heart—

> *You want a partner to witness your life;*
> *a someone I never found, not even / at home—*

Well, Tiger, loneliness is less about being alone than about prowling with the wrong mate in the wrong jungle, where no one knows what's happening in your head.

It's about the yearning to connect with your lost self and retrieve the childhood you never had. Your army officer, role-model father, an illicit lover himself, drilled you to strike at a dimpled object, and nothing else mattered. Life was a job, not a game. For comfort you married the picture perfect swim-suit model daughter of a well-heeled family. But, alas, to no avail.

Then, you peered into "Marlowe's Kaleidoscope" and suddenly an apparent soul mate was *touching sides / of me I never knew.* Hey, we're all alone in this together, Tiger. We can't be saved by someone else's love. We have to love, too. We have to belong to others. Opening up is a great way to show love, but you're right to worry whether that alone will win a fickle heart for a legend like yourself—

> *Will I just be fifth on your list? One more*
> *person who just happens to be famous?*

So the answer was yes, right! That's why loneliness is such a problem for the famous. As Albert Einstein noted, "It is strange to be so universally known, and yet to be so lonely." Loneliness is also the ultimate poverty of the rich. Money can buy all the sex we can afford, but none of the love we need. And, of course, that make-up sex you sent out for isn't love; we've got to create it, not solicit it.

Labyrinths

In this strange labyrinth how shall I turn?

Ways are on all sides, while the way I miss.

If to the right hand, there, in love I burn:

Let me go forward, therein danger is;

If to the left, suspicion hinders bliss,

Let me turn back, shame cries I ought return

Nor faint though crosses with my fortune kiss;

Stand still is harder, although sure to mourn;

Thus let me take the right or left hand way;

Go forward, or stand still, or back retire;

I must these doubts endure without allay

Or help but travail find for my best hire.

Yet that which most my troubled sense does move

Is to leave all, and take the thread of love.

Mary Wroth

John Wareham

MARY WROTH WAS AHEAD OF HER TIME. The sixteenth-century daughter of a powerful, aristocratic, intellectual family, she became trapped in a loveless marriage to a wastrel, spendthrift, drunkard.

She inherited the title of lady, but opted to follow her feminist heart, engage in an affair with playwright Ben Jonson, then take up with her first cousin.

That union produced two illegitimate children and Ms. Wroth fell from social favor. But not on account of the semi-incestuous coupling (which cynics say is popular among English bluebloods). She became persona non grata for publishing a roman a clef, *Urania*, revealing the sexual sins of the powerful of the day.

Aristocrats hate that kind of thing.

This particular sonnet alludes to the labyrinth from which Theseus escaped by following the thread given him by Ariadne. Without that strand, he would have encountered the dreaded Minotaur, a horrible beast, half man and half bull, with a wicked temper and a killer personality.

For sinners, the poet contemplates the maze of sinning love. Turn right and be burned by love? Turn left and miss the pleasure? Turn back and feel impotent? Stand still and mourn? She clarifies her message within the final line: *leave all, and take the thread of love.*

Right on, comrade. Never be afraid to buck convention. True love, even if others see it as sin, will save us.

Or maybe not.

Seductions

My suitor sounds a truly tempting tongue
And teases me with tantalizing lies.
I merely smile and let myself succumb,
Thus feigning innocence of subtleties.
But subtle ties will bind his heart to mine,
And truths untold will overpower my woes,
His chancing eyes for me alone will shine;
I'll have no need of otherworldly beaux.
He'll never flinch or leave me in disgrace,
Nor come to me without a tender show,
He'll always know he won by perspicace,
Seducing me with derring-dainty prose.
In love then, poets are constantly gracious,
Yet all their stratagems quite mendacious.

Elan Haverford

A RAT TRAP NEVER MOVES; IT MERELY WAITS until the rat catches itself. Less obvious is that the trap is a prisoner, too. Lovers exist within such paradigms. To escape they need to reflect that life is transitory and death is certain—and since they're already naked, there's no compelling reason not to follow the heart.

In this sonnet, the poet pretends to be teased and allured by the *tempting tongue* and *tantalizing lies* of her off-limits lover. But, as she candidly admits in the final couplet, she is leading the seduction and attempting to entangle and tame the suitor with *subtle ties*.

If the role of the artist is to make the unconscious conscious, then Elan Haverford might well be unveiling a deeper truth than she realizes.

She might be disclosing the secret intention of more apparently starstruck sinners than we realize. Perhaps, instead of falling in love at first sight, both parties may be guilty, consciously or unconsciously, of entrapping the other to satisfy personal needs?

The assertion in the final couplet, that poets are *gracious* in their work but *mendacious* in their maneuvers, is similar to Haverford's observation in a private letter, "Poets are permitted lies, there'd be no poets otherwise."

Again, Haverford's signature Elizabethan language comes into play, with, *beaux, perspicace,* and *derring-dainty.*

Despite the knowing irony, one gets the feeling, that the poet is vulnerable, perhaps infinitely more so than she realizes, and that the assertion, *He'll never flinch or leave me in disgrace* might just be wishful thinking.

Rodents are never keen to remain entrapped.

Raptures

I'll chance the reckless leap of loving you,

I'll hazard Hero to your Leander;

there'll be no passion I'll not pursue

as your mistress, muse, and courtesander.

We'll sup ruby sunsets and crimson wine,

then nestle on a couch of feather down

to taste sixty-nine raptures, all sublime;

you'll bless my soul, I'll exalt your proud crown.

Dawn will never peep into our domain,

there'll be no sin, no censure, angst, or fuss,

no apprehension of another reign—

just you and me—our own enchanted us.

Above all other writs, ranks love's advice,

so I'll be your love till hell turns to ice.

Elan Haverford

I F WE ARE TO SIN, WE MUST SIN BRAVELY. Illicit love is a blind leap, a spontaneous act, a headlong fall. Perfect judgment is impossible. Devil-may-care audacity is everything.

So, having committed herself physically to the Black Swan—in the earlier sonnet on page 12—the poet now decides to surrender emotionally and spiritually, too. She vows to *chance the reckless leap of loving you*, subtly using the word *leap* as a segue into another mythical story, that of Hero and Leander. Briefly:

> Leander, a young man who lives in Abydos, falls in love with Hero, a priestess of Venus at Sesto. The two cities lie across from each other on the banks of the Hellespont. Every night Leander swims across the strait, guided by a torch that Hero lights on the high tower where she lives. One stormy night, however, the torch goes out and Leander perishes amid the waves. In the morning, after finding her lover's lifeless body on the shore, Hero throws herself from the tower into the sea.

Perhaps the poet sees a similar saltation in store for herself upon casting caution aside to become a *mistress, muse and courtesander*. *Sixty-nine raptures* spells out some of the sensual delights she has in mind; so, too, *bless my soul and cradle your proud crown. Oh, yes, more, please.*

No apprehension of another reign, refers to the other corner of the love triangle; *just you and me—our own enchanted us*, lays claim to a special private realm ruled by the desires of this lusty Leda and her wild Black Swan.

Perhaps, one way or another, for as long as it lasts, all sinners dwell in such a weightless zone.

Shadows

Love is my sin, and thy dear virtue hate,

Hate of my sin, grounded on sinful loving:

O, but with mine compare thou thine own state,

And thou shalt find it merits not reproving,

Or if it do, not from those lips of thine,

That have profan'd their scarlet ornaments,

And seal'd false bonds of love as oft as mine,

Robb'd others' beds' revenues of their rents.

Be it lawful I love thee as thou lov'st those

Whom thine eyes woo as mine importune thee.

Root pity in thy heart, that when it grows,

Thy pity may deserve to pitied be.

　　If thou dost seek to have what thou dost hide,

　　By self-example mayst thou be denied!

William Shakespeare (142)

L OVE CAN BE THE DEADLIEST OF GAMES, which is why life insurance actuarial tables disclose that getting married significantly increases the likelihood of dying a violent death: Frankie shot Johnnie precisely because she loved him, no more so than in the moment of unloading lead into his cheating heart.

But if marriage is formidable, illicit relationships, laden with intrigue and laced with the prospect of tragedy, are even more problematic—as we see in the intricate insights woven into this astonishing sonnet.

We're adulterous lovers, says the poet, but you hate me because I remind you of your own duplicity. Compared to me, you've been sinning for longer, with more off-limits partners, and telling lies to seduce your prey. Even now, when I look lovingly at you, you share come-hither glances with others. This peeves me on one level, but makes you even more alluring on another. I despise you for what you do to me, but I can't help loving you. You'd best be careful, though, because what goes around comes around.

The words *profane* and *scarlet* give a religious cast to an especially intriguing metaphor: *those lips of thine That have profaned their scarlet ornaments And sealed false bonds of love* .... Sure the lips are red, but scarlet is also the color of sin, and on a third plane, the image is of a naughty cardinal dressed in scarlet robes planting forbidden kisses.

The rest shall be left to your imagination.

Friends

If we could be just decorous friends, what a
contented alliance that would be. We
would meet and embrace and keenly murmur
the fond hellos that amiable comrades plea.
We'd be so cheery in our salutations,
so absorbed in sharing our glad stories,
we'd not lament the absent mad infatuation
that provokes the prick of morning glories.
Alas, that pact is not yet sealed, my sweet
and enthralling, clandestine temptation,
for your chancing step whets a rousing sweat,
and then my rapture hot from hell doth run.
So, for now, my love, to friendship cry, Avaunt!
And come with me in Aphrodite's cunt.

Elan Haverford

PLATONIC FRIENDSHIP CAN BE SEDUCTIVE, most men agree on that. In the presence of an attractive female friend they obsessively ponder the prospect of getting lucky. And if such a felicitous opening seems impossible, the friendship generally cools faster than a pizza in an icebox.

Women, on the other hand, sincerely believe in the prospect and value of apparently filial friendships.

Or so they say.

But not, in this instance, anyway, Elan Haverford.

That gift of the sonneteer, to tell a story and extract a startling moral, unfolds genteelly as the poet talks of *decorous friends* in a *contented alliance*, who issue *the fond hellos* and *cheery... salutations* of *amiable comrades*.

The pace accelerates with a flashback to a *mad infatuation* and a subtle—some might say blatant—sexual allusion to *the prick of morning glories*.

Whether the poet is speaking of a former lover or dreaming lustily of an intended triangular love object, is unclear. What is very clear, however, is that the desired swain rouses the poet's passion to the point of *a rapture hot from hell*, and that she wants her intended to forget all about mere friendship, and engage in a passionate clandestine affair.

Needless to say, the initial courtly flavor of the words and phrases dramatically enhances the effect of the heroic couplet, and most especially the last line.

One almost gets the impression of an aristocratic lady who, with the right person in the right circumstances, might delight in venting like a whore.

Fevers

and in moonlight she comes in her nudity,
flashing breasts made of milk-water,
flashing buttocks made of unkillable lust,
and at night when you enter her
you shine like a neon soprano.

Anne Sexton

M IND AND HEART COLLUDE IN A STRUGGLE
that fuses infatuation, enchantment, and lust into
the fever of love.

No passion is so serious, no sickness so potent.

It fells princes, presidents, potentates, and paupers.

Doctors can't quell it. Analysts can't shrink it. Priests
can't expel it. The police cannot arrest it. A spouse cannot
snuff it.

Young men and women sacrifice their lives for it.

Old folks gasp up its beckoning path.

It is a delirium that must take its course.

Games

You said: "To make more sweet that which will be,

Let's play a part together, you and I.

See! I'm a monk, who, in his garden high,

Doth fast and pray to banish things worldly.

Down there you come, sad faced, dreaming of me.

I feel that you 'twixt flowering trees draw nigh;

I look not lest your lips let love flame high,

But, rising, thus I bless you prayerfully."

Señor! That tone! Those gestures strange yet stern!

Tell me, where did you learn them? Tell me true!

Great God, Señor, an unfrocked priest are you!

No, no! No, no! Enough, your kisses burn

Tonight I swear it! You shall be denied,

Grief-stricken glooms o'er us The Crucified.

Edna Worthley Underwood

L OVE IS A GAME THAT TWO CAN PLAY
  and both can win, but illicit love is a dangerous romp
that all too often ends in tragedy. Put such a fate out of
mind, however, for to win anything worthwhile in such dicey
pursuits, one must proceed with abandon.

Which is what happens in this audacious sonnet, one
of many such delights in *The Garden of Desire: Love Sonnets for
a Spanish Monk*, whose passionate anonymous author would
surely be proud of Edna Worthey Underwood's steamy
translation.

Since people are so often the opposite of what they
seem, we perhaps shouldn't be shocked to find, in the first
two quatrains, an apparently holy monk deriving wicked
pleasure by enticing—with a blessing, no less—one of his flock
to fall from grace.

The putative seducee's reply is a masterfully wry. On
one level, she professes confusion:

Señor! That tone! Those gestures strange yet stern!
Tell me, where did you learn them? Tell me true!

On another level, her protestations—*No, no! No, no! Enough,
your kisses burn*—seem disingenuous. And what about the line
following?

Great God, Senor, an unfrocked priest are you!

Golly and gosh—preparing for the basest of missionary
ministrations, the naughty friar has slipped out of his habit—
and his proselyte professes to be shocked. Worst of all, this
naughtiness plays out inside a chapel as Christ on his crucifix
gazes down, grief stricken.

Is this all a little politically incorrect, or what?

As truth inevitably is, of course.

Crossed Lines

Despite the best efforts of my head, my

heart cries out for you, your voice, your body,

the touch of lips, the touch of fingertips,

and an even deeper connection to

your soul: I have crossed lines and I love you.

My heart wants me in your loving arms.

You have a grace and calm that I adore,

sophistication that is so fitting

with your beauty. I could digress and say

you give magnificently gentle kisses;

I love your tan lines; the curves of your hips

the erotic beauty of you holding

yourself in the faded glow of night's light.

Above all, I love your inner beauty.

Mark Sanford

IT HAS ALWAYS BEEN UNWISE FOR SECRET lovers to commit their passions to paper, but never more so than today.

You'd think that everyone would know by now that the *e* in *e-mail* stands for *everyone*. But not, alas, Mark Sanford, former governor of South Carolina and a United States presidential hopeful. An avowedly happily married man and father, and a devout Christian, the governor succumbed to "Marlowe's Kaleidoscope" on a business trip to Argentina, tumbling top-coat over wing-tips in love with a Latin hottie.

He subsequently attended marriage counseling with a Christian adviser, whose predictable advice was to shun the Latina and return repentant to his wife and family. The governor briefly embraced the counsel, but neither distance nor disgrace can lessen the passion of true lovers, and the smitten swain secretly flew to Argentina to spend a clandestine week with his inamorata. Before the love-fest ended, however, the press caught up and the affair made headlines. Then, to the delight of voyeurs, a string of e-mails between the lovers was leaked to the media.

On the bright side, many women were impressed by the governor's romantic mode of expression, and, given his poetic flair, it was a simple matter to distill his exact lines into the heartfelt free verse sonnet opposite.

The sonnet earnestly showcases the governor's heartfelt passion and longing. Given the physical focus, however, the last line might seem disingenuous, or perhaps merely delusional. But, no matter, lovers will empathize, and sinners will, too. For sure, the lines won at least one heart, as, if you will be so kind as to turn the page, you will see.

Ilhabela

I'm reading e-mails in Ilhabela,

thinking of you, watching the sea so blue,

and remembering with a great smile on

my face, the time I have spent with you—

No need to imagine! Just close your eyes

and remember, and I will do the same.

You brought happiness and love to my skies,

and although I don't know if we'll reclaim

that time, or meet again, yet this has been

the best to happen in a long showing.

I don't know how we figure out this scene

and am not interested in knowing.

We will meet again somewhere, sometime, in

this life or next—I'm missing you till then.

Maria Belen Chapur

IN LOVE THE SMALLEST DISTANCE IS TOO GREAT, and the greatest distance can be bridged. So, here's a lover on a faraway beach hoping to tap into the universe so as to become at one with her sinning paramour, physically absent on another continent.

The warmth of the poem is noteworthy. The reader feels what the lover feels; the *sea so blue*, the *great smile* on a beaming face; the delight in *the time I have spent with you*, which, in case we doubt the sexual nature of that trysting, is clarified in the lines, *No need to imagine! Just close your eyes and remember, and I will do the same.*

The heroic couplet, with the suggestion of meeting *somewhere, sometime, in this life or next* seems innocent enough, but the addendum, *I'm missing you till then*, is probably intended to tantalize.

And, if so, succeeded.

Like that of her sinning lover, Governor Mark Sanford, whom we met in the prior sonnet, this is the poet's first published poem, also distilled for these pages from an e-mail, both parties having cast their sentiments into cyberspace.

Perhaps on account of her career as a broadcaster, Maria Chapur projects charm and a feeling for words, so the overall effect is beguiling.

Well, for sure, it enchanted the governor, who chose to risk career and reputation to bridge the distance between his aching heart and his nether regions flame.

Ah, the power of illicit love.

Who can doubt it?

Who can resist it?

Who can survive it?

Fevers

My love is as a fever, longing still

For that which longer nurseth the disease,

Feeding on that which doth preserve the ill,

The uncertain sickly appetite to please.

My reason, the physician to my love,

Angry that his prescriptions are not kept,

Hath left me, and I desperate now approve

Desire is death, which physic did except.

Past cure I am, now reason is past care,

And frantic mad with evermore unrest;

My thoughts and my discourse as madmen's are,

At random from the truth vainly express'd;

    For I have sworn thee fair, and thought thee bright,

    Who art as black as hell, as dark as night.

William Shakespeare (147)

AMAZING, ISN'T IT, HOW A FEW SIMPLE WORDS can convey such complex ideas? The poet tells us he craves more of the opiate—his lover—that is making him ill; he longs for her and wants the fever of love to remain, no matter the cost. He admits that his love is a form of madness, but says he'd rather lose his mind than surrender his lover and regain his sanity.

He says he's babbling like a fool, and that nothing he says makes sense—though, in fact, he's showing profound awareness of, and insight into, his condition.

In the final couplet he may be saying that he made a mistake in judging both the character of his lover and the fever of love itself. He was certain both were *fair and bright*, but now he realizes they're both *as black as hell, as dark as night*.

Maybe, when he regains his senses and gets some therapy, he'll realize that she was just another fallible human being. Given the tone of the poem, however, this patient seems more likely to follow in the footsteps of the poet Rilke, who, upon being advised of the purpose of therapy, immediately quit, explaining, "If they'd take my demons, they'd take my angels, too."

It is intriguing to compare this sonnet with Shakespeare's 129th on page 10. In 129 a detached observer analyses the effects and stages of lust upon sinners generally. Here in 147 we hear a sinner's voice as he struggles within the arc of the malady itself: a pleasure-filled high when entering and ascending, but a nightmare upon landing and alighting.

White Lady

For sure, I grasp the druggist art
you summon to your scene.
You blow me stardust from your heart
and speed the pulsing of my being.
I know your tricks, my courtesan,
the balmy looks that lull my muse,
the sultry smiles that melt my brain,
—I shall trap and sell these subterfuges;
Kings will pay for that cocaine.
And as you float within my sky
beyond all sense of sin,
I note your guise with mellow eyes:
you only play the heroine
to ease the aching soul within.

Chandler Haste

ADDICTION'S A BITCH. SHE COMES WITH A rush upends your world, drives you crazy, then leaves you lying in the gutter begging for more, figuratively, if not literally. Ah, yes, can't get enough of that beautiful, merciless lady.

But what about the woman herself?—*La Belle Dame Sans Merci*, patron saint of sinning addicts—is she an addict, too? Bet your life she is, yes! And *your* life—your body, heart and soul—is the purse for which she plays.

Despite his addiction to her love, or perhaps because of it, the poet says he knows the ingredients of his darling's wickedly appealing powders, and sees clearly how she injects these narcotics into his brain. And, armed with that insight, he admits an intention to patent her potions and sell them—on commission, perhaps.

Modern sonneteers don't always follow formal sonnet structure. Here the poet favors a simpler beat and infuses colloquialisms, especially in the references to sex and drugs—*White Lady . . . blow me stardust . . . speed the pulsing . . . know your tricks."* The line *as you float within my sky,* might also be a sly reference to the Beatles hit, "Lucy in the Sky with Diamonds," slang for LSD.

This would be light verse, save for the final couplet with its neat pun on *heroine.* "You need to drug me," says the poet, "because you, too, are a tortured soul. Outwardly you laugh and play the teasing game of love, but behind all that playacting you're a guilty sinner hoping that the drug of love—and the power it confers—will *ease the aching soul within."*

Takes one to know one, perhaps.

Soul Mates

Our hearts are in tune, we're soul mates, surely,

enjoined upon a spiritual plane;

our love shines intensely and maturely,

'tis the highest form affection can attain.

That's why I so obsess, my love; it's why

you're always in my mind; it's why my brain,

that impassioned voyeur and rabid spy,

roams the tactile landscape of your domain.

So intense is our clairvoyant bond

that when I penetrate your psychic field

I sense you thrill to my spectral wand,

and sigh that love is paradise revealed.

We're sacred angels, my love, soul-locked priests,

anointed to create the two-backed beast.

Chandler Haste

SELF-DELUSION CAN BE VITAL WHEN CITING a soul mate. Most marriages, even happy ones, are mistakes. In a more perfect world, or even with a tad more care in this one, both partners might have chosen more wisely. Once the die is cast, however, society insists, and those joined accept, albeit often ambivalently, that one's soul-mate is the person to whom one is actually married.

But sinners go on looking, and the divining instrument with which they hope to identify the absent perfect partner is seldom located in the heart.

In this sonnet, the sinner opens with the avowal that he and his new best friend enjoy soul-mate status within a spiritual plane, where their love *shines intensely and maturely* in the *highest form affection can attain.*

In the second quatrain, the tone tilts to the sensual, perhaps even the bawdy. It's because our love is so pure, says the sinner, that my brain becomes a voyeur and lingers over conjured images of your *tactile landscape.*

The third quatrain ups the ante. Spiritually we're already coupling, says the sinner; *when I penetrate your psychic field / I sense you thrill to my spectral wand.*

Finally, the poet's underlying goal is disclosed; he has been joshing, perhaps hoping that his blend of sly humor and poetic skill will seduce the putative soul mate. He finishes with a disingenuous non sequitur; it is precisely because we're *soul-locked priests,* he says, that we've been *anointed to create the two-backed beast.*

Divinely selected to conjugate!

God works in wondrous ways.

Swan Song

A sudden blow: the great wings beating still
Above the staggering girl, her thighs caressed
By the dark webs, her nape caught in his bill,
He holds her helpless breast upon his breast.

How can those terrified vague fingers push
The feathered glory from her loosening thighs?
And how can body, laid in that white rush,
But feel the strange heart beating where it lies?

A shudder in the loins engenders there
The broken wall, the burning roof and tower
And Agamemnon dead.

                                Being so caught up,
So mastered by the brute blood of the air,
Did she put on his knowledge with his power
Before the indifferent beak could let her drop?

William Butler Yeats

IF FANTASIZING ABOUT RAPE IS A SIN then wicked thoughts need to be sanitized for publication. So, at first glance, Yeats's "Leda and the Swan" explores mystical ideas and retells the mythical rape of Leda by the god Zeus in fine-feathered form, thereby siring Helen of Troy, whose beauty led to the destruction of that early Greek civilization.

But a peek into history suggests that the sexy sonnet is also a rape fantasy that eased the poet's unsated lust for Maud Gonne, a militant Irish nationalist.

The poem opens with the fowl attack and the maidenly terror. The rhythm in the lines evokes the violence of rape, and as in most male fantasies *loosening thighs* open to the rapist's charms. Fortunately the assault happens within a sonnet so the crime is bridled and brief. After ejaculation comes dramatic silence. Then, later, the poet ponders the meaning of it all.

Ah, Billy, it was about your Madonna-Whore hang-up. You kept a fancy girl down in London for whoring and enjoined in a "spiritual" marriage with the icy Madonna-figure, your fellow mystic Maud. But you *also* believed that spiritual love must be fulfilled by, uh, coition. You sublimated your lust into a work of art but still obsessively pursued the apparently unattainable Maud. A decade later she granted you a nightmarish one-night stand. Neither of you could respect the other in the morning; the Madonna fantasy went the way of your *indifferent beak*—and with it the relationship, too.

But at least the self-therapeutic sonnet lives on.

We should all be so lucky.

Longing

The village I dwell in, Thinkingofyou,

is a maddeningly melancholy town,

where the clocks are locked in a strange snafu

and the forget-me-nots are hand-me-downs.

Clandestine lovers crave sweet rendezvous

but I chance the night streets, alas, in vain,

for lanes are manias in Thinkingofyou

that sun-bolt beams are inept to unreign.

Folks never slumber in Thinkingofyou,

in the mornings we do not wake either,

we lie in a state we dare not adieu,

valedictions merely fan our fever.

Thinkingofyou is the sweetest of jails

but I pray reprieve lest sanity fails.

Elan Haverford

IF TORTURED TO REVEAL A VITAL SECRET, no captive terrorist could withstand the level of pain that sinning lovers routinely inflict upon each other.

And if wavering sinners apprehended the level of suffering about to come their way, they'd turn and run for their lives—for the potency of that pain is sufficient to contaminate an entire existence.

That level of torment pervades this intense sonnet, which has been hailed as Elan Haverford's finest.

The striking central idea, that obsessive love is a *maddeningly melancholy town / where the clocks are locked in a strange snafu*, appeals on several levels.

The sinner's ambivalence toward her role of Other Woman is touchingly, and one imagines, honestly, reflected in the image of *forget-me-nots* that are *hand-me-downs*.

Hoping to ease her cravings for her absent lover, she seeks him by traipsing through the *night streets*, and continuing her search until the *sun-bolt beams* of morning strike. By that time, however, she has descended into such a state of wretchedness that she fears for her sanity.

She would like to end the relationship, but admits that attempts to say good-bye only make things worse; *valedictions merely fan our fever*

The multilayered meaning of the eleventh line, *we lie in a state we dare not adieu*, is noteworthy. The sinner admits to being a liar, as is the norm in clandestine relationships; she indicates that the state of her consciousness is also a problem; finally, one can only *lie in state* after death (that ultimate Land of Might Have Been where illicit love is legitimized, and poets are always immortal).

Judgment

They say that they who've sinned this sin of ours

May never after death know aught of light;

Naught can once cleanse their souls,

                       nor make them white,

Nor Lydian scents make sweet the sin-stained hours.

A gate whose whirling swords have lightning's powers

To blast and burn flash outward with such might

The black and barren road is bleached to bright

That leads down, downward,

                       where the darkness cowers.

Come, Sweet, lift up your eyes! Be not afraid.

Behold! within that pit a giant rose,

Its million, million petals, hearts of those

Who sinned this sin of ours all undismayed,

So rich, colossal, glorious, and fair

It dims the white sword-whirl of judgment there.

Edna Worthley Underwood

A FELICITOUS REWARD IN THE NEXT LIFE, for those who live exemplary lives in this one, would be permission to flit, according to one's mood, between heaven and hell; heaven for the comfort, hell for the companionship.

This might seem a particularly apt outcome for a supposedly celibate monk doing God's work by day, then, fulfilling the sexual, perhaps even spiritual, needs of an ardent parishioner by night.

Elsewhere in her anthology, *The Garden of Desire*, the poet displays a modicum of conflict and guilt. Ultimately, however, she is mostly, as in this particular sonnet, ingloriously unrepentant.

Here, she scorns the pious believers who say that blatant sinners like herself and her black-frocked swain are on a *black and barren* road to hell.

Come, Sweet, lift up your eyes, she says. Behold! within that pit a giant rose. A rose whose million petals contain the hearts of those / Who sinned this sin of ours all undismayed.

From sinner's perspective, the heroic couplet is decidedly dauntless. There can be no judgment in hell, she avows, to compare to our *rich, colossal, glorious, and fair* love for one another.

Well, so she hopes.

For in that hope lies sinners' bliss.

Forget regret, they say, or life is yours to miss.

Rightly or wrongly, it is an appealing idea.

Shame

Last night unto my bed bethought there came
Our lady of strange dreams, and from an urn
She poured live fire, so that mine eyes did burn
At the sight of it. Anon the floating flame
Took many shapes, and one cried: "I am shame
That walks with Love, I am most wise to turn
Cold lips and limbs to fire; therefore discern
And see my loveliness, and praise my name."
And afterwards, in radiant garments dressed
With sound of flutes and laughing of glad lips,
A pomp of all the passions passed along
All the night through; till the white phantom ships
Of dawn sailed in. Whereat I said this song,
"Of all sweet passions Shame is the loveliest."

Alfred Douglas

SHAME IS THE ACCOMPLICE WHO GUARDS the door to the secret lives of sinners. Shame seldom springs from personal mistake or social faux pas. Rather, it is a sense of abasement that flows from feeling that we have no choice but to be what we are, and that this ignominy is apparent to everyone. The paradox here, the tragedy, actually, is that the vital thing in life is to live the authentic life of the person you truly are.

Alfred Douglas—"Bosie" to his friends—was the notorious lover of Oscar Wilde. Bosie's famous line, "I am the love that dare not speak its name," penned in an earlier poem, became synonymous with homosexual love, at that time a criminal offense. The liaison destroyed Wilde, costing him two years at hard labor, from which he never fully recovered.

As we see here, however, like so many poets, Bosie delights in exploiting his most intimate foibles; the *shame that walks with Love* comes to him in a dream and tells him to *see my loveliness and praise my name.*

Times have since changed. Gay pride has arrived, gay marriage is a fact, and the love that dare not speak its name is sung in chorus atop rooftop gardens.

For everyday adulterers, however, the edgy stain of shame might provoke *A pomp of all the passions passed along / All the night through,* but would they award it top billing—*Of all sweet passions . . . the loveliest?*

Probably not.

And so, even for dedicated sinners, a love that dare not speak its name lives on.

Lamentations

To pass through life with a soul that has never known sorrow,
is to be ignorant of one half of nature.

Seneca

IMPALED UPON THE CRUCIFIX OF ILLICIT LOVE, sinners discover themselves between two thieves—guilt and desire. Worse, however, than the inescapable presence of these lamentable companions, is the agony of the ungovernable, intermittent absence of the loved one.

Indeed, for clandestine lovers, coming together may be easier than getting together. And, of course, whenever they encounter one another in public, they have to seem, as the title of the country song has it, "Strangers When We Meet."

Such subterfuges command a costly psychic price.

So is the game truly worth the candle?

Only a sinner can say.

But how's a scamp to rationalize such sinning without seeming too hypocritical?

Calling one's lust, love, and then avowing that love is the most sacred of human gifts is a stratagem favored by most, hence Oscar Wilde's observation, "They do not sin at all / Who sin for love."

Perhaps even Jack the Ripper could excuse his excesses by explaining it was merely human nature.

Doldrums

My paramour belongs in other places,
and trims his words to suit a distant peal,
and marks the dipping sun beyond my graces,
and flees from me as shadows prick his heel.
Imprisoned time flees fastest when I'm doting
upon the vision of my love before my lips,
aboard a haunted craft so wanly floating
upon a doldrummed sea of empty ships.
If he were mine, and mine alone forever,
intensity of love might subtly waive,
so bind these blinding moments to me ever,
to shimmer from within a mirrored grave.
Superior then, I say, is lust in haste
to sanctioned love and ever-lost embrace.

Elan Haverford

COPIOUS INTELLIGENCE AND IMAGINATION are invested in self-deceit because the need to maintain an illusion is deep.

Here, for example, the poet attempts to extract an upbeat conclusion from an unhappy state of affairs.

She opens with the wan but honest observation that her lover censors himself out of concern for his marriage vows, gazes past her to other obligations as the day passes, and then runs back to his betrothed as sunset falls. At that point, for the poet, time halts. Now, silent, alone and going nowhere—like Coleridge's Ancient Mariner *upon doldrummed sea*—she reflects upon her vision of her hastily departed paramour.

An ambivalent, wistful undercurrent, is neatly expressed in the line, *flees from me as shadows prick his heel*, with the word *prick* hinting at sexual interest of the swain in both relationships, and both *prick* and *heel*, characterizing him as a cad.

The extent to which the poet is distressed by feelings of rejection and guilt, might be signified by the hint of suicide as she suggests that she will soon enough *shimmer from within a mirrored grave*.

In the hope of easing these feelings, she offers an intriguing rationalization, which she doubtless wants to believe, but within the recesses of her heart probably does not: inevitably and subtly, marriage causes love to fade, so brief, lusty assignations are better.

Dedicated sinners would doubtless agree.

But, really, what do they know?

Absence

How like a winter hath my absence been

From thee, the pleasure of the fleeting year!

What freezings have I felt, what dark days seen!

What old December's bareness every where!

And yet this time remov'd was summer's time,

The teeming autumn, big with rich increase,

Bearing the wanton burden of the prime,

Like widow'd wombs after their lords' decease:

Yet this abundant issue seem'd to me

But hope of orphans and unfathered fruit,

For summer and his pleasures wait on thee,

And thou away, the very birds are mute;

Or, if they sing, 'tis with so dull a cheer

That leaves look pale, dreading the winter's near.

William Shakespeare
(97)

LOVE IS A LABYRINTH OF PARADOXES. To love someone is to pine in their absence yet also to draw comfort from feeling close in heart.

Illicit love, however, spiked as it is with the apprehension that all may come to a sudden end, is rather more precarious.

So, for a lonely sinner, whatever the season, the absence of one's lover, seems like an unending winter. And, here, the poet plays with that idea, saying:

> Spring—the prime season—was followed by a summer
> that produced a rich increase of teeming leaves. For
> me, however, there can be no summer without you,
> and because you were absent I personally suffered a
> dark and freezing winter.

Intriguing here, is the lush image of *widow'd wombs after their lords' decease*. One's lover is absent, but the person who remains is pregnant with the anticipation of a new summer.

Alas, however, so long as the absence endures, that anticipation is merely an orphaned hope, for *summer and his pleasures wait on thee*.

It is so dull and dreary without you, says the poet, that even the birds are unhappy, and, goddammit, here comes winter again.

Inflammations

Clandestine love, my love, was the only

love we ever had. I ached for more of

course. Did you? *Yes* . . . but you whisper softly,

leaving me befuddled and unsure of

your teasing tongue. There's always the lover

and the loved, and I'm the spellbound former,

always yearning for more than to hover,

an ill-fated moth as you brightly shimmer.

I pine in your firmament, burning to

bind us together, touch you everywhere,

taste you all honeyed and gold, to and fro,

then kneel to murmur the silken prayer

that flowers the pip in the secret briar....

Ah, covert love, my love, inflames such desire!

Chandler Haste

SINNERS HANKER FOR WHAT THEY CAN'T HAVE. In this case, the poet pines for more than love in the shadows. He worries that instead of loving him with the same intensity that he feels for her, his secret sweetie might just be stringing him along, even as she plies him with sexual delights.

One might wonder whether the observation, *There's always the lover and the loved*, might apply equally to sinners and angels. Perhaps that imbalance of affection might be even more prevalent among married partners than cheating duos.

The mutual magnetism of the clandestine affair, is after all a rather special gravitation, a key element of which is that both partners assume significant risks in order to spin within the other's orbit.

Here, perhaps recognizing that his life could go up in flames at any moment, the poet compares himself to an *ill-fated moth*. That lust is a prime attraction for him is apparent in the desire to *taste you all honeyed and gold*. And having made that confession, the poet descends even further into the overtly and wildly sexual.

But I am not to blame for my excesses, he adds, exclaiming, *covert love, my love, inflames such desire!*

True enough, secrecy bestows a special gift, even as it takes and destroys so much of everything else.

But what the hell?

So says the sinner.

Angels and Sinners

Two loves I have of comfort and despair,

Which like two spirits do suggest me still:

The better angel is a man right fair,

The worser spirit a woman color'd ill.

To win me soon to hell, my female evil

Tempteth my better angel from my side,

And would corrupt my saint to be a devil,

Wooing his purity with her foul pride.

And whether that my angel be turn'd fiend,

Suspect I may, yet not directly tell,

But being both from me, both to each friend,

I guess one angel in another's hell:.

    Yet this shall I ne'er know, but live in doubt,

    Till my bad angel fire my good one out.

William Shakespeare
(144)

WITH AN ANGEL PERCHED ON ONE SHOULDER and a devil lurking on the other, it's no wonder sinners wind up schizoid. What might be telling in this poem, is that the devil comes in female form. She's Jezebel, Lilith, Carmen and every other Beautiful Lady Without Mercy who ever tempted any ill-starred male.

The poem tilts in the third quatrain with the poet's confession that he can't figure out whether the bad spirit has succeeded in corrupting his good angel:

> . . . *whether that my angel be turn'd fiend,*
> *Suspect I may, yet not directly tell;*

The trouble is, says the poet, that since both angels are part of me, they're on friendlier terms than ideal ones—and might even have become lovers:

> . . . *being both from me, both to each friend,*
> *I guess one angel in another's hell:*

I can't know for sure whether, the good angel has plunged his member into the female pit, but if so the hell of syphilis will surely follow. Till then, I must wait:

> *Yet this shall I ne'er know, but live in doubt,*
> *Till my bad angel fire my good one out.*

Right! There being no penicillin in Elizabethan times, the bad angel will ultimately, uh, discharge the fiery residue of the good angel.

Oh, that William Shakespeare was sooo bawdy.

Tête à Tête

Perhaps I'll come to live inside your trousers—

As a rare pair of knickers—would you dare?

Living there would be so much easier—

Oh, Freddie easier than falling off a chair.

I do so want to feel my way along you—

Oh, God you're good, so come you surely may—

In and out, and up and down upon you—,

We need a night to set us on our way.

So pray, my Gladys, destiny will sway.

A night alone with you?—fate come find me!

A night of love, if you know what I say.

I'd suffer anything, that's love, you see.

So pray for fate to set us on our way—

You're a clever old thing, that's what I say.

> *Charles Windsor*
> *and Camilla Shand*

INTIMACY IS ALL ABOUT REVEALING SECRET thoughts and creating a unique shared memory bank of roses, dinners, wines, songs, books, plays, movies, pet names and magic moments.

How disappointing then, for British subjects to discover, upon the release of the intimate cell phone conversation from which this sonnet is distilled, the limited vocabulary of their lovesick heir apparent.

As a courtesy to poetry lovers, infamous references to proprietary feminine hygiene products are omitted, but the sentiments and words—and playmate monikers—are otherwise authentic.

The sonnet opens with the nobleman's proffer to reside within his mistress' undergarments. Well bred lassies might find such déclassé overtures off-putting. Not this accomodating courtesan, however, who shows a shrewd appreciation of the fish she hopes to land. Every man wants to believe himself an irresistible lover, and she casts this fly adroitly and unremittingly.

Whereas he dwells sophomorically upon her private parts, she appeals to his fragile ego—*Oh God you're good*—and the notion that fate will preserve their love. She also neatly casts herself in the role of victim; *I'd suffer anything, that's love, you see.*

She sets him up so cleverly that he becomes a willing accomplice to his own deceit. Finally, with the easy calm of a loving comrade, she numbs his brain with a dosing line: *You're a clever old thing, that's what I say.*

Not so clever at all, alas. A gentleman in love may behave like a lunatic, but, please, not a vulgarian.

Needs

I, being born a woman and distressed

By all the needs and notions of my kind,

Am urged by your propinquity to find

Your person fair, and feel a certain zest

To bear your body's weight upon my breast:

So subtly is the fume of life designed,

To clarify the pulse and cloud the mind,

And leave me once again undone, possessed.

Think not for this, however, the poor treason

Of my stout blood against my staggering brain,

I shall remember you with love, or season

My scorn with pity,—let me make it plain:

I find this frenzy insufficient reason

For conversation when we meet again.

Edna St. Vincent Millay

WOULD ANY MODERN MALE EVER DARE attempt such a poem? Only a woman, surely, could so callously confess her intention to seduce some hapless Mr. Close-Enough for no other reason than to sate her lusty appetite.

By way of excuse, she claims to losing the fight *against the poor treason / Of my stout blood against my staggering brain.* The male version of this plea is that a standing member has no conscience. It's a notion that doesn't play out terribly well with the PC crowd—or even many male magistrates, these days. But, for sinners, anyway, it's a refreshingly honest piece of work (as you are, too, Milady).

The moral of the sonnet, is equally direct: "Just because I gave in to my desires, doesn't mean I left my mind in a jar by the door. So don't make the mistake of thinking I will remember you with any affection just because we, ah, conjoined. Next time we meet, my brain will be in charge, so don't even try to engage me in conversation."

Goodness! Can you imagine the heartbreak of the poor swain who after being bewitched and abandoned by sweet Edna St. Vincent Millay, got to read these lines?

Oh, Edna, come back, come back from wherever you are!

We just love your poetry.

And your haughty manner.

And your stiletto heels and whip.

Encore!

More please—of *everything*.

Onlookers

'Tis better to be vile than vile esteemed,

When not to be receives reproach of being,

And the just pleasure lost, which is so deemed

Not by our feeling, but by others' seeing.

For why should others' false adulterate eyes

Give salutation to my sportive blood?

Or on my frailties why are frailer spies,

Which in their wills count bad what I think good?

No, I am that I am, and they that level

At my abuses reckon up their own;

I may be straight though they themselves be bevel;

By their rank thoughts, my deeds must not be shown,

   Unless this general evil they maintain:

   All men are bad, and in their badness reign.

William Shakespeare
(121)

AH, BUT IF ONLY NAUGHTY BILL CLINTON, forty-second President of the United States of America, had known, he might have recited this superb sonnet to silence the sanctimonious scolders of his sexual proclivities, and thereby dodged impeachment.

"If I'm to suffer for a sin," says the poet, "then I should at least have the pleasure of committing it. I'd rather be an out-and-out sinner and get a full measure of lusty pleasure, than merely be thought to be a sinner, and enjoy nothing.

"I confess that *I am what I am*—a high-spirited fellow—so I won't defend the indefensible risings of my *sportive blood*. I refuse, however, to tolerate the hypocrisy of mealymouthed critics who get their sexual jollies by imagining all the fun they think I'm having (and spoil for me the little bit of whoopee I might be having).

"These mudslingers are liars and worse. Their *rank thoughts* and *adulterate eyes* sinfully violate the privacy of the special relationship between myself and my lover. When they tout my imagined peccadilloes—*level / At my abuses*—they're simply *reckoning up* their own vile fantasies. So don't try to judge my behavior through the prism of their foul minds; *By their rank thoughts, my deeds must not be shown*, unless, they care to admit that we're all sinners, even the high and mighty among us."

Sinners and scholars who enjoy Shakespeare's predilection for spicing his stuff with bawdy double-entendres might note the eighth line, where the words *will* and *count*, Elizabethan slang for the male and female genitalia, rub up against each other.

Farewells

And ever has it been known that love knows not its own depth until the hour of separation.

Kahlil Gibran

FEELINGS HEIGHTEN IN MOMENTS OF FAREWELL. A lover's last goodbye kiss, that pensive reverse greeting, can seem, in the moment of turning away, to have masked the delivery of a dagger into the heart.

But let us not be starry-eyed; yes, sinners do fall out of love, and when that happens good-byes can come as a welcome relief.

For ever-loving sinners, however, those blessed—or cursed—by what songwriter Christine Lavin memorably called "The Kind of Love You Never Recover From," partings are tragedies, and every hint of farewell is a foretaste of death.

So, even when such sinners exchange overtly well-intentioned farewells, they never truly mean for anything to end; distance and time fail to loosen the bond, and nothing truly changes.

Kind Cuts

"I don't want to hurt or abandon you
—so what to do?" you ask. Well maybe first

drop me into a pot of boiling glue
then have a witch doctor apply a curse.

Or when that fails and I rise in pursuit
of you, have a firebug set me aflame.

Or cut out my tongue and render me mute
then poke out my eyes and publish my shame.

Or, here's aptly felicitous fate
for this hopelessly addicted lover:

Bobbitting!—that could be the kindest bite
to slice me out from under your thumb of.

Off the top of my head that's my advice,
Bow to it gently, and in love, rejoice.

Chandler Haste

D ENIAL IS ONE WAY TO HANDLE REJECTION,
humor another. Here, sensing that his lover's words
I don't want to hurt or abandon you, in fact flag her underlying
intention to end their affair, the poet blends nonacceptance
with wit.

For the classic sonnet form to deliver such modern
drollery might seem unusual, but the funny stuff masks a
couple of rather more serious messages.

First, the poet is saying, You're joking, of course; please
don't seriously consider quitting our affair, to do so would
be torture for me.

Second, the reference to *Bobbitting*, whereby Lorena
Bobbitt infamously removed her husband's member with
a carving knife, is funnier, when, in the third quatrain, one
catches the ambiguity of the words *felicitous* and *bite*.

A follow-up invitation—*Off the top of my head*—comes in
the opening line of the heroic couplet, and instructions on
precisely how the lover should pull that off that are clarified
in the final line.

The sensibility in play might not seem Shakespearean,
but Mr. Haste may have picked up some tricks from the
bawdy master.

Dreams

Farewell, thou art too dear for my possessing,

And like enough thou know'st thy estimate:

The charter of thy worth gives thee releasing;

My bonds in thee are all determinate.

For how do I hold thee but by thy granting?

And for that riches where is my deserving?

The cause of this fair gift in me is wanting,

And so my patent back again is swerving.

Thyself thou gav'st, thy own worth then not knowing,

Or me, to whom thou gav'st it, else mistaking,

So thy great gift, upon misprision growing,

Comes home again, on better judgment making.

>   Thus have I had thee as a dream doth flatter:

>   In sleep, a king, but waking no such matter.

William Shakespeare
(87)

CLASS ANXIETY MIGHT JUST BE AN ENDEMIC British malady, but anyone with a shaky sense of self-esteem will probably identify with the poet's message, "You're just too upper crust for me, and now we both know it. I tricked you into loving me early on, when you didn't realize what an aristocrat you truly are—or maybe you didn't realize that compared to you, I'm just a lowlife. Whatever. It was just a dream, and it's all over now."

Of poetic note, is the unusual endline repetition of the suffix *-ing*, which evokes feelings of melancholy and monotony. And all but one of the lines have eleven syllables instead of the conventional ten. Perhaps, by quitting tradition the poet intends to highlight his message of farewell. The reliance on legal language—*charter . . . patent . . . misprision . . . estimate . . . worth . . . bonds . . . riches*—might also hint at a decree of divorce.

The heroic couplet is intriguing. On one level, the poet says that only after the breakup did he realize that his love affair was just an unsatisfying illusion. And, now, he finds no redress in reality, either; the clear light of day exposes the chasm that separates himself and his lover, and always did.

On another level, the melancholy mood is lightened by a bawdy double entendre. "I tupped you—*had thee*—as in as in a wet dream," says the poet, "In sleep I, too, was an aristocrat, *a king* with power to command your love. Upon *waking*, however, I realize I'm just a nobody, so a person of your high rank could never truly conjoin with me in real love, hence, *no such matter*."

Tissues for tears only, please.

Promises

I never lamented nor even sighed

for you; I never whined, whimpered, or wailed;

No tear was shed, no incipient tide

of melancholy brine was ever bailed.

So tender no nauseous, giddy good-byes,

bear no mawkish sentiment on your sleeve,

feign no fervor in those fine feckless eyes,

neither delay, nor distrust, nor reconceive.

Run from me, chancelessly, hastily, leave;

spring from me, speedily, ever so quick;

swiftly, remorselessly, end this upheave,

flee from me, fly from me, smoothly and slick.

But as you retreat down the trail of time,

Promise you'll ever and always be mine.

Elan Haverford

TO BECOME HAPPY WE NEED TO FORGET, but to do so we need to engage the mind in anamnesis— reaching back into memory—and when we do that we all too often engrave unhappy thoughts into the brain.

On the bright side, memory feeds imagination, and for this poet, anyway, melancholy recollections have produced a nifty sonnet.

In proclaiming so boldly he has forgotten all about her, the poet joshes in the hope of catching her attention, amusing her, and winning her back. He also offers up hints of desire—*you may feel encountered . . . you are strictly undone*— designed to tickle her fancy.

The image of *a slice of your Venetian blind peepers in my mental masquerade ball*, suggests a voyeuristic, masked lover sneaking forbidden glances.

The heroic couplet ratchets the sexual ambiguity to another level.

On the surface, *To spin on that shaft you haven't a chance* says you're prohibited from waltzing me around my mental dance floor.

Subliminally, however, the poet raises the prospect of his former lover whirling once more upon his own shaft—and says he'd be delighted to accommodate such dervishings should she so desire.

Right now, however, she seems to be out of his orbit, so he might well be reduced to mental reruns of past, um, circumductions.

Ah, yes, God gave us memory so we can have roses in December.

Corridors

So, now that I'm completely over you

I await the wireless phone to ring

and get a buzz from what's not happening,

for you, indeed, are blocked and can't get through.

And, since I do not even think of you

when casually glancing at your photograph,

I merely note the fading autograph

and that your countenance is dimming, too.

Oh yes, I am completely over you:

I do not stare down shady corridors,

or dream of clandestine forbidden shores,

or other zones I'm not supposed to view.

Ah, yes, my life is better through and through

now that I am completely over you.

Chandler Haste

SINNERS ARE LIARS AND LOVERS ARE, TOO. Lack of self-insight being normal among sinners, especially those of the lusty variety, they don't always know what they're saying.

Ultimately, however, when the breakup comes, reality peeps in through the cracks, as we see in this sardonic sonnet.

In asserting, *I'm completely over you* the poet's overbright mask and over-the-top protestation reveal an ongoing obsession with his departed flame, and shares more than a little heartbreak, as he waits forlornly, hoping against hope for the phone to ring and e-mails to arrive, all the while doting upon a photo of his former flame. We are left to suppose that neither this image, nor the signature beneath it are fading, only the prospect of ever being reunited.

The ambiguous references to *shady corridors . . . clandestine forbidden shores*, and *other zones I'm not supposed to view* suggests a reluctant, almost mournful semi-acceptance of an unwanted chalice of reality laced with an insoluble shot of lingering desire.

An unwelcome medicine, for sure.

Kiss and Part

Since there's no help, come, let us kiss and part,

Nay, I have done, you get no more of me,

And I am glad, yea, glad with all my heart,

That thus so cleanly I myself can free.

Shake hands for ever, cancel all our vows,

And when we meet at any time again

Be it not seen in either of our brows

That we one jot of former love retain.

Now at the last gasp of Love's latest breath,

When, his pulse failing, Passion speechless lies,

When Faith is kneeling by his bed of death,

And Innocence is closing up his eyes,

Now, if thou wouldst, when all have giv'n him over,

From death to life thou might'st him yet recover.

Michael Drayton

FALLING IN LOVE TAKES A MILLISECOND, but when the flame of passion fails, rekindling it—or effecting an adroit farewell—can be tricky. And in such moments character is revealed.

This sonnet is similar in some respects to "Corridors" by Chandler Haste on page 74. The difference is that this particular pining lover—in real life a glum and discontented lifelong bachelor—casts himself as a victim.

The sonnet opens with a decidedly passive-aggressive send-off: "*Since there's no help, come let us kiss and part,*" he says: "*I am glad, yea, glad with all my heart* to be free of you—and if we meet again, it'll be as perfect strangers, who *not one jot of former love retain.*"

Then, in a sudden switch, the poet invites the lover he has so icily abandoned to imagine a scene in which Love is in the last throes of dying on a deathbed surrounded by a triumvirate of mourners; *speechless Passion, kneeling Faith,* and *Innocence closing up his eyes.*

There is good news, however. Even in this *last gasp of Love's latest breath:*

> *if thou wouldst, when all have giv'n him over,*
> *From death to life thou might'st him yet recover.*

Yes indeed—Love *can* be rescued. All the belittled and shafted lover needs to do is surrender a sweet glance, a soft word, a fond sigh of love, whatever. Then Love will come to life, and make-up sex will doubtless follow.

Don't fall for it Baby.

He's a surly loser.

Kick the bum out.

Dialysis

There may be other worlds—you said there were—

yet, trapped in empty rooms, I atone

to strangers whose insipid lips chauffeur

a tedious cargo of pumice stone.

And there, reclining upon alien

shoulders, sit you, my love, inconstantly.

You're my erstwhile dialysis machine,

enlivening me even as you weigh

me down, being now there and now not there,

your presence reminding me only of

your absence. Oh, yes—you fled our affair,

escaped my eyes, if not our hand in glove.

There may be other worlds in which we're docked,

but all the passages, my sweet, you locked.

Chandler Haste

LONGING, THAT DESPONDENT ACHE OF unrequited love, is never enough for serious sinners. They pine for the thrill of slipping convention's bonds, the titillation of secret trysting, the mainline fix of the loved one's worshipful gaze, the tingling balm of clandestine lovemaking.

Go cold turkey on all of that, and pangs of withdrawal follow. Here, the poet grieves the ultimate absence of his lover. Life became lifeless. Friends became strangers whose *insipid lips*, instead of conversation and kisses, merely *chauffeur / a tedious cargo of pumice stone.*

The luminous memory of his lover, floating in and out of consciousness, serves only to remind him of her truancy. Having no alternative supposedly clears the mind, but not for this forlorn poet: dote as he might upon his missing lover, he cannot escape Krishnamurti's observation:

> In the space which thought creates around itself
> there is no love. This space divides man from man,
> and in it is all the becoming, the battle of life, the
> agony and fear.

Even though she's gone, his heart wants to believe they're still connected, still *hand in glove*. What his head tells him, however, is the affair really is over, and that she has locked him out of her life.

A nice sonnet, honest, serious, melancholy, and distressed.

Time wounds all heels, alas.

Endings

*He remembered the dissolute adventures in which his senses,
his nervous system and his mind had indulged; he saw himself
corroded by irony and intellect, laid waste and paralyzed by
insight, almost exhausted by the fevers and chills of creation,
helplessly and contritely tossed to and fro between gross ex-
tremes, between saintly austerity and lust—oversophisticated
and impoverished, worn out by cold, rare artificial ecstasies,
lost, ravaged, racked and sick—and he sobbed with remorse
and nostalgia.*

Thomas Mann

SECRECY HEIGHTENS A SINNER'S PLEASURE,
but with it comes the apprehension that a bad beginning
makes a bad ending, and a nagging level of anxiety and guilt,
which typically torpedoes the affair.

At that point, guilt-wracked sinners feel relief, but
dedicated love addicts suffer a sense of loss and longing.

For them, if the opening act was a heart-stopper, the
closing curtain can be a soul destroyer.

On the bright side, the ending of sorrow can be the
beginning of wisdom.

Well, maybe.

Treatments

I will swallow strong pills to conquer love's

ills, and remove you at last from my thoughts.

You will exit my brain and that nervous

membrane will suffer no further onslaughts.

You'll melt into exile, as will your sweet

smile, so, too, your tilting, half-lidded eyes.

Oh yes, you'll depart, my mind and my heart,

all trace of fateful vivace exorcized.

The doctor's ambrosia will hasten all

closure, for sure it consummately will;

my brain will be surging with mind-numbing

purging, if only I'll stay on the pills.

Well, so I imagine before I weep,

tossing and turning in my troubled sleep.

Chandler Haste

DOCTORS PRESCRIBE TRANQUILIZERS for lovesickness, so, if this poet wants to try that kind of *mind-numbing / purging*, pills are obtainable.

On the downside, however, chemical remedies ignore underlying causes, arresting both delight and distress along with the lessons pain can teach. Let's be honest, if Shakespeare had been on Prozac his love sonnets would have turned out differently, and by now they'd all be gracing gushy greeting cards.

So, what's a better cure?

Tilt your eyes leftward.

To attempt a sonnet, or letter to oneself, can be highly therapeutic—and in this case probably was.

The poet knows he's not making sense, of course; he knows his doctor is lying; he knows he'd rather grieve than swallow such pills. Down deep, he also knows that *closure* is just a silly, specious word, and that he'll never truly forget his vanished flame.

Intuition is telling him that he must extract something worthwhile from his otherwise wretched breakup.

So, poetic license being what it is, he opens with a big lie—that he's hoping to treat his pain with analgesics—and closes with the reality that loosing and turning and tears are more infinitely comforting; that opening the briny ducts clears the way for heart and mind to rescue something lasting from distress.

And, of course, that something saved might just be a sonnet like this one, where, despite all the joshing, internal rhymes tumble like tears.

Reconciliation

The world saw someone struggling. None of us
is perfect. We are all trying to do
the best we can. I also feel sorry
for the other woman. I am sure she
is a fine person, though I do sometimes
question her judgment. But all I can do
is pray for her, because she made some poor
choices. Mark made some poor choices. People
were brought down. All I can do is forgive.
Reconciliation is something else,
and that is going to be a harder road.
It's up to my husband to do the soul-
searching to stay. The ball is in his court.

Jenny Sanford

Reaching out to sinners is never easy, and all too often unwise—as might be true of this sonnet distilled from a magazine interview given by Jenny Sanford, wronged wife of Mark Sanford, the sinner whose sonnet to his mistress we contemplated on page 30.

It helps to reflect that as heiress to an industrial fortune, Jenny Sanford's money and power effectively installed her husband in the governor's mansion.

One would expect him to be eternally grateful, but those who marry for money mostly enter into an arrangement wherein they earn every last cent: they sign on as financial partners, and, try as they might, seldom truly come to love anything but lucre.

Love sonnets typically display passion and intellect, ideally both. But not this one. The word *love* never gets a mention. The tone is cool and detached, and, though it pretends to be otherwise, the thrust is condescending and judgmental.

Most crucially, compared to the speaker in Shakespeare's thirty-fifth (on page 104), this wronged spouse shows no interest whatsoever in considering how her own judgment or behavior might have been suspect.

The heroic couplet neatly summarizes the poet's case: the philandering husband's soul needs to be examined, and the ball is in his court.

To compare the tone of this wronged partner's attempt at reconciliation with the mistress's missive (page 34) is to fully grasp the power of illicit love.

Don't count on that ball coming back into play, Jenny.

Hearts

Being a princess isn't all it's cracked up to be.

I didn't want gifts or fancy wages,

just to be queen of hearts and then decree

love for the unloved to last for ages.

I never needed a golden carriage;

all I wanted was someone there for me—

but there were three of us in that marriage,

a bit of a crowd, I'm sure you'll agree.

Life's just a journey, we all wind up dead,

So I wore my heart on my sleeve and led

from the heart, not the rule book of the head:

if you find love, Hang On, is what I said.

Yes, be a free spirit, hear your heart sing

Or call on me, and I'll come running.

Diana Spencer

FOR A CLEAR-EYED HEIR APPARENT, MARRIAGE is an arrangement to protect land, money, and power. A bride must be virginal, fecund, and, ideally, passive. So, on a putative prince's wedding day, a supposedly royal family invited the world to witness a supposedly joyful exchange of supposedly sacred vows.

Alas, however, it was all a depressing fairy tale wherein an emotionally paupered prince blithely betrayed both the doe-eyed bride at his side and his tearful paramour watching from the pews.

Oh, Diana, in saying, *all I wanted was someone to be there for me*, did you not realize the rules of the game? Did you truly believe that your prince would be different from any other? Did the Queen not explain that with the chore of marriage out of the way, a prince in need of love and intellectual companionship is always entitled to a mistress?

No need to respond. Your sonnet, distilled from your words, is answer enough. You succumbed to illusions conjured by avaricious aristocrats and obsequious clergy fawning for power and position.

You believed in romantic love. What you didn't realize then, is that love is a flower that blooms best in secret—which is why your prince's passion lay elsewhere.

To be fair, your apparent naiveté is becoming the new world standard. Honesty is starting to win more plaudits than hypocrisy. But nothing is easy, and modern couples demand so much from marriage that partners inevitably come up short.

But we hear your message.

When we find love, we'll hang on, too.

Secrets and Lies

Hey! The story's a lie, a tabloid scam:
I have always been in love with the same
warm, loving, beautiful, sexy woman;
we share a steadfastly abiding flame.

Okay! I had a lapse, a short affair.
It happened when she was in remission.
I shared my mistake and begged forgiveness,
and she forgave, that's her disposition.

Look, I was a boy, an upright small-town lad
who soon became a national public name.
Listen, I'm not the first person to do bad,
but it was *wrong*—and I'm to blame.

I might've lost that boy along the way,
but the affair's long over, let me say.

John Edwards

SINNERS FALSIFY FOR FEAR OF MISSING OUT on love; then, spurred by a sense of shame, they go on lying because there seems no other viable option.

In this sonnet distilled from media conferences called by the former trial attorney and South Carolina senator John Edwards, he forthrightly "clarifies the facts" concerning his alleged extramarital affair with a political groupie.

The poem opens with what turned out to be a bald lie, then proceeds to an avowal of marital constancy discordantly laced with the word *sexy*.

The second quatrain is an ambivalent mea culpa. The poet admits to *a lapse, a short affair,* a *mistake* for which he begged and received his wife's forgiveness—perhaps because, being a gentleman, he sinned only when her cancer *was in remission.* Now comes the clincher: "Success and fame caused me, an upright small-town boy, to lose my moral compass."

At this point, one might be inclined to overlook the whiney tone and absolve this semi-contrite sinner. Who much cares, after all, whether he loves his wife? Or whether his affair was more than a one-nighter.

But the heroic couplet is just too clever. The sinner says he *might've* lost a little innocence, but immediately launches into yet another lie, for soon enough, as the world discovered, the affair was fully ongoing.

So, there it is: dissembling becomes so ingrained that sinners lose both the capacity to tell the truth and contact with reality, which ultimately overtakes them.

Wiser, perhaps, if backed into a corner, to offer up the entirely credible lines of Ernest Dowson, "I have been faithful to thee, Cyrana, in my fashion."

Rings

I said, I don't need jewels or rings

I just want you to be faithful. You see.

I just don't care for material things,

so I merely asked for fidelity.

Then this woman stalked him, he said, and, yes,

I wanted to know details. So, fine,

"You're so *hot*" is what she said, he confessed.

Well, *I* could *never* deliver that line—

that person is *so* different from me.

Yes I've seen a picture of the baby:

It doesn't look like mine, on that we agree.

Her being so strange was enticing, maybe?

Do I still love? It's a complicated vow;

but I can't wear my wedding ring right now.

Elizabeth Edwards

THOSE WHO SEEK TO IMPRISON LOVE with a demand for fidelity fail to appreciate that desire is a bird that seldom survives in a cage.

In this sonnet, distilled from an Oprah Show taped in the poet's twenty-eight thousand square foot home, the narrator confides her reaction to the dalliance of her husband, a former United States presidential contender, whose passionate campaigning delivered a professional loss and a personal love child.

In the opening, the poet notes that she's frugal soul who *merely asked for fidelity*. And, alas, all she got was a fast-talking attorney who rendered them rich arrivistes. When the pledge didn't pan out she *wanted to know the details*. So we learn that the lover was seductive in ways the poet could never be. In labeling the progeny *It* and noting *that person is so different from me*, the poet showcases a level of anger at odds with her public persona. The heroic couplet also shows more ambivalence than insight, but the final line is revelatory.

Existentialists would say that the poet hoped to create meaning by binding herself to an upward striver. But such strivers typically crave more adulation than one partner can provide, and also carry the seeds of self-destruction. By torpedoing his career this husband also annihilated his wife's life purpose. So, at age sixty and dying of cancer, Elizabeth ditched the ring and shared her story with America's High Priestess of Love Relationships, thereby bequeathing an enduring tale of betrayal to the world, and a rich legacy of ongoing heartache for her husband, his tootsie, and *It*.

Ah, Love.

Equations

Consider the equation of my life:

the formula's abjectly all awry,

fortune's fast falling, apprehension's rife,

what'ere I do I diabolify.

The trickster on the stage is vaulted time,

who casts a trance of momentary daze,

so exit from his pointless pantomime

and gather in the next world all bouquets.

Roll the fickle dice and seize the chances,

ride on to colliding parallel worlds,

disdain all pain of darkling nuances,

impasses implode as valor unfurls.

My spirit to another Globe has flown,

yet rests within your palm to claim your own.

Elan Haverford

DEATH PUTS A SUDDEN END TO SINNING but poems can live forever—and poetic narratives from the grave are not unknown, the most noteworthy being Shakespeare's sonnet 71, *No longer mourn for me.* Elan Haverford's "Equations," however, may be the only suicide note ever cast in sonnet form.

And a lovely farewell it is, blending her fondness for antique words—*abjectly . . . diabolify . . . trickster . . . vaulted . . . fickle*—with subtle multilayered allusions: *vaulted time* suggesting time trapped in a tomb; *momentary daze*, suggesting both passing bewilderment and a neat pun on *days* that are fleeting.

Of interest, in this moment when she takes her life, is that she seems courageous and upbeat as she considers the conundrum of her life and loves—and prepares to *exit a pointless pantomime . . . ride on to colliding parallel worlds there to gather all bouquets*—this later phrase perhaps being an oblique reference to what she hopes might be an otherworldly capacity to sight her own funeral flowers.

That she truly believes that the world is pointless, however, seems contradicted in the final couplet. Now, in a subtle shift of tense, she says she has already departed one Globe theater—a neat Shakespearean allusion—and landed in another. In so doing, she lays a clever claim to immortality—the first requirement of which is death—noting that her spirit, this very sonnet, no less, *rests within your palm to claim your own.*

Brilliant, yes, as a means to end a love affair, but recommended only for the intellectually ambitious.

Chances

In the dream, your soul sought the sky before

you did, and started to soar of its own

free will; free in the moment it foreswore

the throng to fly to a fortune unknown.

Inspired by that courage you followed suit,

flouting the doubts of inhibiting friends,

gliding past cynics in unbound pursuit

of the helix your heart said ascends

to the life you've been chosen to live,

from the moment you commit to embrace

the heartfelt pleas of that soul-starved plaintiff

whose appeals you'd persistently debased—

until your chancing heart fled for the clouds

resolved to save the only life it could.

Chandler Haste

FOLLOW YOUR HEART—IT SOUNDS SO EASY. Just takes courage, right? Here the poet tells of a premonition pushing him to bypass *the doubts of inhibiting friends*, and go with the *heartfelt pleas* of intuition.

Trouble is, it was just a dream.

So let's ask an honest question: upon waking, which takes the most courage, staying grounded or soaring toward the unlived life of one's dreams?

By way of answer, let's first reflect that it is infinitely easier to be a lover than a partner. A lover is an inconstant playmate, there for the secret trysts, the wine and the roses, the thrills and the delights. A partner, however, day in and day out, is called upon to be an adult, and to share the bills, strifes, frustrations, and tragedies.

So, in taking flight, one not merely off-loads a partner, but maybe also loses the very lover one had hoped to win—and perhaps becomes embroiled in a stew of not so appetizing in-laws.

The favored fun and games that were meant to last forever, and for which a partner was sacrificed on the altar of love, may never get going again.

No, no, you say, I know my lover well, and my love is so deep that I truly know we were meant to live together. Not so fast, says Voltaire, "If you think you love your mistress for herself, you are mistaken." Right, that apparently fair and bright lover, may actually be, as noted earlier, "as black as hell, as dark as night."

Ah, love, why so many sides to a triangle?

What's the problem, really?

Souls

Poor soul, the centre of my sinful earth,

Rebuked by these rebel pow'rs that thee array,

Why dost thou pine within and suffer dearth,

Painting thy outward walls so costly gay?

Why so large cost, having so short a lease,

Dost thou upon thy fading mansion spend?

Shall worms, inheritors of this excess,

Eat up thy charge? Is this thy body's end?

Then, soul, live thou upon thy servant's loss,

And let that pine to aggravate thy store;

Buy terms divine in selling hours of dross;

Within be fed, without be rich no more:

    So shalt thou feed on Death, that feeds on men,

    And Death once dead, there's no more dying then.

William Shakespeare
(146)

SINNERS ARE INGENIOUS FINGER POINTERS, but this sonnet takes the blame-game prize, for the narrator berates neither wife nor lover, but his own soul:

> *Why dost thou pine within and suffer dearth,*
> *Painting thy outward walls so costly gay?*

"And why," he asks, "do you lie around whining and wasting so much of my precious time and money chasing fleeting earthly indulgences?"

> *Why so large cost, having so short a lease,*
> *Dost thou upon thy fading mansion spend?*

"Worms will eat my body, so as I approach death, which seems ever closer these days, shouldn't you be trying to secure a place for the two of us in the afterlife, by extracting something of value from my profligate, wicked, earthly ways?"

> *live thou upon thy servant's loss,*
> *And let that pine to aggravate thy store;*
> *Buy terms divine in selling hours of dross;*
> *Within be fed, without be rich no more:*

A subliminal message throughout the poem is that sinning eats through cash faster than worms through a corpse; almost every line contains a word or phrase relating to money or debt.

"Rent and maintenance of the sweet life is costing me a bundle, so change your ways. Escape Death's eternal doom by forgoing the sweet life for the decent life—*Buy terms divine in selling hours of dross.*"

The beauty of this sonnet, is that the sinner is free to get on with his sinning. It's only his soul that has clean up its act.

Epiphanies

I believe in the forgiveness of sin
and the redemption of ignorance.

Oscar Wilde

IT IS IMPOSSIBLE TO TRULY KNOW THE ENSLAVING power of illicit love without having first been incarcerated within its crazy penitentiary.

Only by serving real time in love's prison do the inmates come to experience deliverance; only then can illusion be superseded by de-illusion, only then can perception displace passion.

It is as true of a lover as of love itself; we only know well the paramour to whom we so madly committed—then, later, objectively judged.

Anyone who has never succumbed to the enchantment "Marlowe's Kaleidoscope" remains as blind to reality as the hapless lover still spellbound.

Yes indeed; to understand the intensity of illicit love one must be free of it, but not always have been free. Only then can we appreciate the potential alchemy in situating. with luck, that intoxicating experience can be transmuted into wisdom, which, if it does not bring joy, can yet bring happiness.

Potions

What potions have I drunk of Siren tears,

Distill'd from limbecks foul as hell within,

Applying fears to hopes, and hopes to fears,

Still losing when I saw myself to win!

What wretched errors hath my heart committed,

Whilst it hath thought itself so blessed never!

How have mine eyes out of their spheres been fitted,

In the distraction of this madding fever!

O benefit of ill, now I find true

That better is by evil still made better,

And ruin'd love when it is built anew

Grows fairer than at first, more strong, far greater.

    So I return rebuk'd to my content,

    And gain by ill thrice more than I have spent.

William Shakespeare
(119)

HERE'S A SONNET FOR LONG-SUFFERING innocents who hope for the day when their cheating partners see the light, repent their wicked ways, and return to hearth and home, never to tryst at the Other Corner again.

Yes, such a metamorphosis is possible, and such a day may come, says the poet, apparently drawing upon painful personal experience. And, best of all, he explains, a sinner's fulsome fevers and torrid tears can ultimately lead not just to enlightenment, but to an infinitely greater life and love for the one he seemed to forsake.

The poem opens with a confession: "My unreal-ism, pain and self-destructive behavior sprang from my own inner mental imbalance and emotional wounds—an unholy mixture *distilled from limbecks foul as hell within*"—(an alembic being a distilling apparatus, often used creating gin or whiskey). So loaded, the hapless sonneteer careened from one self-delusion to another, *Applying fears to hopes, and hopes to fears, / Still losing when I saw myself to win!*

His fever was so great, it was as if someone had plucked out his eyes. He ultimately discovered, however, that all this darkness and distress—and evil—served to nurture rather than destroy his capacity for love. And that the love he thought he had ruined could be regained, then flourish into something even greater.

Maybe so, but some sinners, too many perhaps, are incapable of real love, so forgiveness doesn't always lead to healing.

Not that a serious sinner would care.

Recognitions

Upon ruminating the mystery

in my staggering run of rotten luck,

and mulling my puzzling history

of shining dreams reduced to sullen muck,

I conjured surly saboteurs corrupt

who schemed, alas, to scuttle every goal

invoking cunning curses to disrupt

the stars that held my fortune in control.

Then a plaintiff entered my reflection,

whose inverted visage made me shiver,

for the eyeballs that coerced connection

condemned the countenance in my mirror.

Yet if I'm creator of all my strife

I can also fashion a whole new life.

Chandler Haste

LIKE LOVE ITSELF, ENLIGHTENMENT SEEMS to appear suddenly and unexpectedly. But don't be fooled. Within the secret shadows of desire, our minds and hearts have been conspiring, for God only knows how long, to deliver the insight that will set us free.

Here, as he gazes into a mirror, the poet's confession to *ruminating the mystery / In my staggering run of rotten luck*, seems wry, as if intuition is already discounting luck as the source of his problems. So, too, the second quatrain, we sense the heart doubting the existence of *surly saboteurs* or *stars that held my fortune in control*.

At this point, the poet's own mirrored image locks onto his eyeballs, and in the courtroom of conscience, condemns his transgressions.

Yes, of course! We create, by our own attitudes and actions, our own realities.

And, now, comes a blinding flash of the obvious.

> *if I'm creator of all my strife*
> *I can also fashion a whole new life.*

In that moment of enlightenment, sinners face a moment of truth and set about making some hardheaded decisions.

Cowards will seek and follow the counsel of one-dimensional, so-called spiritual counselors, whose advice will never vary: "Forswear thy foolish ways, and live according to your personal obligations and social conventions."

Only the most courageous saints and reconstructed sinners will dare to embark upon the challenge of creating the life they truly believe they were meant to live.

Thieves

No more be griev'd at that which thou hast done:
Roses have thorns, and silver fountains mud,
Clouds and eclipses stain both moon and sun,
And loathsome canker lives in sweetest bud.
All men make faults, and even I in this,
Authorizing thy trespass with compare,
Myself corrupting, salving thy amiss,
Excusing thy sins more than thy sins are.
For to thy sensual fault I bring in sense—
Thy adverse party is thy advocate—
And 'gainst my self a lawful plea commence.
Such civil war is in my love and hate
    That I an accessary needs must be
    To that sweet thief which sourly robs from me.

William Shakespeare
(35)

THE BEDEVILING CATCH WITH ADULTERY is that it requires an accomplice. In identifying that coconspirator most aggrieved partners point the parental digit of a clenched fist to the Dark Lover in the Other Corner. In so aiming, however, three fingers point back at the accuser. That, on one level, is the message of this subtle sonnet, which, had he known her, Shakespeare might have dedicated to Hillary Clinton.

The opening line, *No more be griev'd at that which thou hast done*, seems utterly forgiving, but the next three turn increasingly peevish, comparing the handsome partner's sexual weakness—perhaps even his male member—to a thorny rose, a muddy fountain, and a loathsome canker.

"*All men make faults*, and so do I," adds the poet. "In so kindly comparing your sins to those of others—*authorizing thy trespass with compare*—I'm corrupting myself. I'm the wronged party, but you, you son of a bitch, you've reduced me to the demeaning role of unprincipled advocate charged with the brief of lying to save your seamy skin by *Excusing thy sins more than thy sins are.* I love you and hate you both. Worse, I blame myself for forgiving and defending you, you wormy two-timing rogue."

Well said. But if love involves endless acts of forgiveness, there are ulterior motives: by absolving a straying mate, the aggrieved party hopes to defeat the Dark Rival by reclaiming the roving cad's affection; forgiveness can also be an act of revenge, excorcizing the Dark Rival, and lobotomizing the errant partner.

Some would say it seemed to work for Hillary.

Springs

In my dream an inner spring came rising

up through clandestine aqueducts to drench

and thus revivify the dry and dying

garden that all my tears had failed to quench.

Then I saw a glorious beehive hover-

glide above my mulish melancholies,

and golden bees, like jubilant lovers,

confecting honey from my past follies.

Lastly, a chastening sun fired fiery darts,

annihilating my losses and lies,

absolving my crimes, healing my heart

and cleansing the salt from my scarlet eyes.

Into my blindness these images crept

redeeming my sight as I softly wept.

Elan Haverford

SEEKING TO FORGET INGRAINS HEARTACHE: it is through the filter of anguished memory that redemption is distilled. Get into enough trouble, experience enough pain, guiltily reflect for long enough, and then absolution rises through remorse, ever so slowly, from within the deepest recesses of the heart.

And, as in Elan Haverford's sensitive sonnet (inspired, surely, by the late Spanish poet Antonio Machado) the messages a transgressor needs to receive, seep into consciousness during sleep.

Psychotherapists say that a dream that's not been analyzed is like a letter that's not been opened. But poets are also seers, so this particular dreamer is keenly aware that her startling chimera is revealing that she has been irrevocably changed.

An eternal *inner spring* has flooded her psyche and absolved the sins that tears alone could not erase.

The second set of images—a *glorious beehive* gliding above her distress, and *golden bees, like jubilant lovers, confecting honey from my past follies*—heightens the sense of transformation.

Third, come *fiery darts* from a rising sun, *absolving my crimes, healing my heart / and cleansing the salt from my scarlet eyes.*

The poet's unspoken crimes are subtly suggested in the words, *clandestine* and *follies*, and the thrill of reclaiming sight from the blind passion of a secret affair is nicely captured in the heroic couplet.

We should all be so lucky.

Honor

My muse now happy, lay thyself to rest,
Sleep in the quiet of a faithful love,
Write you no more, but let these fant'sies move
Some other hearts, wake not to new unrest.
But if you study, be those thoughts addressed
To truth, which shall eternal goodness prove;
Enjoying of true joy the most, and best
The endless gain which never will remove.
Leave the discourse of Venus, and her son
To young beginners, and their brains inspire
With stories of great Love, and from that fire,
Get heat to write the fortunes they have won.
And thus leave off; what's past shows you can love,
Now let your Constancy your Honor prove.

Mary Wroth

HAVING NOTHING BUT THE DEVIL'S LEAVINGS to offer God, sinners often acquire "virtue" as they age, and offer "good advice" as consolation for being unable, sadly, to partake of carnal pleasures.

So, in this final sonnet in a "crown" of fourteen, after first living a scandalous life, Mary Wroth comes to preach the "womanly" virtue of constancy. What begins as a "farewell to love" addressed to her muse, turns into a *hasta la vista* to immature love, for both herself and her lover. To maintain her integrity she has abandoned him—and he should forgo sinning, too.

It's time to grow up, and discard the fantasy of love, she says. Refuse to accept Cupid's charms, however powerful, as an excuse for irresponsible behavior. Only then, she says, can her swain become the man of honor she knows him to be. Best of all, in embarking on that journey, he'll find, as she has, that constancy brings a union with the divine.

Let's be honest, this is good advice, even for atheists. Only cynics might note that when our vices desert us we flatter ourselves that we're deserting them. Or as the Bard observed:

> Youth is nimble, age is lame,
> Youth is hot and bold,
> Age is weak and cold,
> Youth is wild, and age is tame.

Yes of course! The caliginous clouds that trail every sinner's voyage have the proverbial silver lining: there's no need to hurry to avoid temptation; old age will rob us of it soon enough.

Ghosts

What lips my lips have kissed, and where, and why,

I have forgotten, and what arms have lain

Under my head till morning; but the rain

Is full of ghosts tonight, that tap and sigh

Upon the glass and listen for reply,

And in my heart there stirs a quiet pain

For unremembered lads that not again

Will turn to me at midnight with a cry.

Thus in winter stands the lonely tree,

Nor knows what birds have vanished one by one,

Yet knows its boughs more silent than before:

I cannot say what loves have come and gone,

I only know that summer sang in me

A little while, that in me sings no more.

Edna St. Vincent Millay

MAYBE CHEKOV WAS RIGHT: "IF YOU ARE afraid of loneliness, don't marry." Having fallen into matrimony late in life, Edna St. Vincent Millay seems to agree, claiming consolation in having bedded many lovers.

Indeed, on what biographers say was her wedding night, she writes of hearing a ghostly gathering of past paramours tapping at her window, and laments that:

> in my heart there stirs a quiet pain
> For unremembered lads that not again
> Will turn to me at midnight with a cry.

The message—that the poet was wise to flout convention by sleeping around—is not a philosophy that wins a warm welcome among today's pious PC police.

But if there are chords within us that need to be struck by other people—and if, as Kafka observed, the meaning of life is that it ends—then it might be okay for sinners to savor a myriad of liaisons before *in winter stands the lonely tree*.

The poet, as a young woman, was the verdant tree in which the summer sang; the birds were her joyful lovers, the boughs her inviting bed.

Now, however, the winter of her life has arrived; she is alone, the birds are gone and the *summer that sang in me . . . sings no more*.

In real life, Millay and her husband had just committed to an "open" marriage, so perhaps that has something to do with why she draws comfort in reflecting that she was once passionate and desired.

For sure, anyway, the haunting melody of her many past illicit loves lingers on.

Streets

I dance the field in Saturnalian state
and blind to danger fall into a grave;
dishonored, I chastise uncaring fate,
but rebound back again to misbehave.
Swaggering one dawn, I scoff into that pit
—but then, as in a spell, a devil's tail
flares forth, incensing me, and thus I slip
and helpless plunge into that fiery bowel.
Contrite, I glimpse a sprite above my eyes—
the light of steadfast love! I heavenward reach,
then gently float into emerging skies,
and glide to rest upon a sandy beach.
I watch the dawn depart the rising sun
and, wiser now, in other fields I run.

Chandler Haste

THE DEVIL WHO DRAGGED DON GIOVANNI to hell may have been hoping to claim the soul of this poet, too. But that's not what happened, for as we discover, this sonnet of redemption relates a journey from nightmarish dancing with the devil to blissful ascension into heaven.

The poem opens with an arrogant sinner, blinded by lust, tumbling into several of poetry's figurative graves—fiery feminine wells, probably, but liquor bottles, too, perhaps. It is also a journey from the blindness of wicked pleasure to the enlightenment of steadfast love.

There's ambiguity in the notion of *a devil's tail* flaring forth, *as in a spell*. If that tail belonged to a sensual she-devil, we're not surprised that a mere male member perked up, tempting its aroused owner to plunge into a fiery bowel.

Contrition is followed by enlightenment as the poet glimpses the power of "steadfast" love. Then as he gropes heavenward toward it, he finds himself delivered from his formerly wicked ways.

As usual, the heroic couplet contains a profound message. As the sun arises on a new day, the poet's new-found enlightenment effects a change in his actual behavior:

> I watch the dawn depart the rising sun
> and, wiser now, in other fields I run.

Right! The path to peace is created not discovered. Intention is vital, but it is what we *do* that matters most.

Actions alter us and our destinations, both.

The Pole Star

Let me not to the marriage of true minds

Admit impediments: love is not love

Which alters when it alteration finds,

Or bends with the remover to remove.

O no, it is an ever-fixed mark

That looks on tempests and is never shaken;

It is the star to every wand'ring bark,

Whose worth's unknown, although his height be taken.

Love's not Time's fool, though rosy lips and cheeks

Within his bending sickle's compass come,

Love alters not with his brief hours and weeks,

But bears it out even to the edge of doom.

    If this be error and upon me proved,

      I never writ, nor no man ever loved.

William Shakespeare (116)

IN THE PLAYGROUND OF ILLICIT LOVE the game is seldom what it seems. At first glance this sonnet innocently exalts the constancy of love, but the incessant allusions to bending, removing, height, lips, and cheeks might also slyly invoke male bedroom prowess. Perhaps the most intriguing take, however, is that some jilted Jenny (see page 84) is rebuking a cheating spouse who dared declare, "you're no longer the person I fell in love with, and I've changed, too, so I'm leaving."

To catch the pain and ire in Jenny's rebuttal, add emphasis to the word *me* in the opening—*Let me not to the marriage of true minds / Admit impediments.* Now, add emphasis to the next thought: *love is not love / Which alters when it alteration finds.* Then go to the fifth line and add emphasis and an exclamation mark: *O no! It is an ever-fixed mark /That looks on tempests and is never shaken.*

Such a tone, might not bring your errant spouse home, Jenny, but he might just ponder the notion that he has only briefly veered off course, and that if his love is real he'll return. He might also realize, no matter what havoc time has wrought, your own inner strength has not faded, and, come morning, the midnight lips and cheeks of a trolling trophy might not seem so rosy.

"But I'm utterly torn between two lovers," a sinner may respond, "so how do I know which to choose?"

Okay, then. Close your eyes and imagine both paramours standing before you, smiling sweetly, arms wide open. Now, without thinking, let your arms reach out for the one you most want to embrace.

Then race that soul mate off to heaven.

Guilty?—Let those
Who know not what a thing temptation is,
Let those, who have not walked as we have done,
In the red fire of passion, those whose lives
Are dull and colourless, in a word let those,
If any there such be, who have not loved,
Cast stones against you.

Oscar Wilde

Index of First Lines

Let me not to the marriage of true minds 114

Love is my sin, and thy dear virtue hate, 22

My love is as a fever, longing still 34

My muse now happy, lay thyself to rest, 108

My paramour belongs in other places, 50

My suitor sounds a truly tempting tongue 18

No more be grieved at that which thou hast done. 104

Our hearts are in tune, we're soul-mates, surely, 38

Perhaps I'll come to live inside your trousers– 58

Poor soul, the center of my sinful earth, 96

Should I o'er leap the tempting Rubicon 12

Since there's no help, come, let us kiss and part, 76

So, now that I'm completely over you 74

The expense of spirit in a waste of shame 10

The village I dwell in, Thinkingofyou, 42

The world saw someone struggling. None of us 84

There may be other worlds,—you said there were— 78

They say that they who've sinned this sin of ours 44

'Tis better to be vile than vile esteemed 62

Two loves I have of comfort and despair, 36

Upon ruminating the mystery 102

What lips my lips have kissed, and where, and why, 110

What potions have I drunk of Siren tears, 100

You said: "To make more sweet that which will be, 28

You want a partner to witness your life, 14

Contributors

Maria Belen Chapur, a native Argentinian, works as a journalist and translator of English in the Argentine television station Canal America. She is fluent in several languages, and widely traveled, but this is the first time her poetry has appeared in English.

Michael Drayton was born in Warwickshire, England in the mid sixteenth century. Little is known of his early life, but he was friends with famous men of the age, including Ben Jonson and William Shakespeare. A restless and discontented poet, he produced much and won some critical acclaim. His style is mostly turgid, however, and he is mostly remembered only for the outstanding sonnet included in this anthology.

Alfred Douglas was born in 1870, the third son of the Marquis of Queensberry. He attended Oxford University, was a keen sonneteer, and became lover to Oscar Wilde, a liaison that resulted in the imprisonment of the playwright for homosexuality. In 1923, Mr. Douglas lost a suit for libel brought by Winston Churchill, and served six months in England's austere Wormwood Scrubs Gaol. He died in 1945.

Elizabeth Edwards was born in 1949, the daughter of a navy pilot. She earned degrees in arts and law, then married John Edwards in 1977. They are the parents of four children, the first of whom was killed in a car accident in 1996. Subsequently, at age forty-eight and then again at fifty, apparently after harvesting the eggs of a younger woman, she gave birth to two children. Elizabeth practiced law before joining in her husband's political campaigns. In 2004, she was diagnosed with breast cancer. In May 2009, she released a book, *Resilience: Reflections on the Burdens and Gifts of Facing Life's Adversities* in which she discussed her husband's infidelity.

John Edwards was born 1953 in South Carolina. The son of a mill worker, he completed a law degree in 1977 and married. He earned a substantial fortune as a personal injury lawyer, then entered the political arena. He was selected to run as vice president on the 2004 Democratic ticket. After losing that race, he briefly sought the 2008 Democratic presidential nomination. In the course of that failed campaign, he engaged in a liaison that produced a love child.

Chandler Haste, the rebellious son of a Dorset endocrinologist, received a degree in psychology from Columbia University in New York, where, in 1974, claiming to be a "reborn existentialist," he took American citizenship. Perhaps by way of compensating for a physical disability, he became an organizational psychologist, a field which provided insights for his poems concerning the issues of overachievers. His poetry and a fictionalized version of his persona first appeared, allegedly without his consent, within the 2004 novel, *Chancey On Top*. He is married to Jillian Amicus, a former teacher and sometime actor.

Elan Haverford, said to be the daughter of a British viscount, was born in 1955 and apparently raised in various British colonies. Little is known of her private life, but her sonnets – five of which were published within the novel *Chancey On Top*–suggest that she partnered with a married lover in an affair that ended tragically, with her suicide in the south of England in 1980.

Edna St. Vincent Millay, poet and playwright, was born in Rockland, Maine, in 1892. In 1912 Millay's poem "Renascence" was published, bringing her immediate acclaim and a scholarship to Vassar, where she enjoyed lesbian status. She moved to New York's Greenwich Village to pursue a Bohemian life. In 1923 her fourth volume of poems, *The Harp Weaver*, was awarded the Pulitzer Prize. That same year she partnered in a sexually open marriage, which ended with her husband's death in 1949. She died the following year.

Jenny Sanford, heiress to the Skilsaw fortune, was born and raised in Winnetka, Illinois, and holds a bachelor's degree in finance from Georgetown University. Before becoming a full time mother, and then a poet, she was a Wall Street executive, and a political operative.

Mark Sanford enjoyed careers in finance, real-estate and politics, rising to become governor of South Carolina and to be considered as possible 2012 Republican presidential candidate—perhaps, as we have seen in this anthology, on account of his natural warmth and flair for fine language.

William Shakespeare is best known for the Elizabethan era plays and sonnets attributed to his name. Little is known of his actual life. Some critics sense that his was merely a generic "brand name" assigned to the work of notable others. According to this philosophy the sonnets ascribed to him were possibly written by either Edward de Vere, Earl of Oxford, or Christopher Marlowe—whose editorial sensibility is believed to be intrinsic to the plays.

Camilla Shand, born in London in 1947, the daughter of a British army officer, attended British private schools, then finishing school in Switzerland. An avid equestrian she also enjoyed fox hunting. She was married to a British military officer from 1973 to 1995, but most of that time was also mistress of Charles Windsor, whom she eventually married in 2005.

Diana Spencer, ex-wife of Charles Windsor entered into a tempestuous affair with a cuckolding redheaded army captain, who is said to have fathered her rebellious redheaded son, currently in line for the British throne. A troubled individual but a self-proclaimed free spirit, she enjoyed connecting with the poor and sick. She died in 1997 at age thirty-six following a high-speed crash in the limousine of an Arab playboy, while fleeing paparazzi.

Charles Windsor, an eldest son, was born in 1948. Judged by his domineering father to be overly delicate, Charles was sent for "toughening" to austere all-male boarding schools in Scotland and Australia. Despite mediocre grades he was admitted to Trinity College, Cambridge, and was awarded a rare lower second-class bachelor of arts degree. He subsequently served in the British navy and air force. Bearing the title of Prince, in accordance with royal tradition, he bedded numerous British citizens before marrying, first Diana Spencer, then his long-term mistress Camilla Shand.

Edna Worthley Underwood, born in Maine in 1873, was raised in Kansas, graduated from the University of Michigan, and worked in New York. She wrote novels, plays, poetry, prose, short stories, and news articles. Her original works include novels *The Whirlwind*, *The New World Trilogy*; a collection of essays, *A Book of Dear Dead Women*; and two volumes of poetry, called *Improvisations*. She was fluent in six languages, and received numerous awards for her translations. She died in 1961.

Eldrick Tont "Tiger" Woods, the only child of a retired United States Army lieutenant, was born in Cypress, California on December 30, 1975. A golfing prodigy, his achievements rank him among the most successful golfers of all time, and the highest paid, permitting him to establish charitable projects. He married a former Swedish model and au pair, and the union produced two children. In 2009, seventy-two hours after a tabloid magazine claimed that Woods had been party to an extramarital affair with a nightclub manager, he had a car accident and suffered facial lacerations. After over a dozen women subsequently claimed to have enjoyed liaisons with him, he admitted "infidelity." Perhaps in keeping with his cool persona and poetic gifts, he "believes in Buddhism . . . Not every aspect, but most of it."

Mary Wroth, born in 1587, was a poet of the Renaissance and a pioneering feminist. A member of a distinguished literary English family, she was among the first female British writers to achieve an enduring reputation. She is perhaps best known for having written *The Countesse of Mountgomeries Urania*, the first extant prose romance by an English woman, and for *Pamphilia to Amphilanthus*, the first known sonnet sequence by an English woman. She died in the early 1650's.

William Butler Yeats was born in 1865 in Dublin, Ireland. He was a pillar of both the Irish and British literary establishments and a two-term Irish senator. He pursued a lifelong interest in mysticism, spiritualism, occultism, and astrology. In 1889, he met and fell into an obsessive infatuation with Maud Gonne, an heiress, ardent nationalist, and fellow mystic, eighteen months his junior. His subsequent love interest was Olivia Shakespear, whom he met in 1896, and parted from one year later. In 1891, Yeats proposed marriage to Gonne, but was rejected, at which point, he later noted, "the troubling of my life began." He again unsuccessfully proposed to Gonne in 1899, 1900, and 1901. In 1903 she married an Irish nationalist, but the friendship with Yeats persisted. Finally, in Paris in 1908 they consummated their relationship, then, virtually immediately, ended it. Twenty years later Yeats recalled that only sexual tryst they shared in his poem "A Man Young and Old":

> My arms are like the twisted thorn
> And yet there beauty lay;
> The first of all the tribe lay there
> And did such pleasure take;
> She who had brought great Hector down
> And put all Troy in wreck.

Acknowledgments

My thanks to the sonneteering angels and sinners whose poems made this voyage possible: my angel wife, Margaret, but for whose support and encouragement this work might never have seen the light of day; ever-daring Welcome Rain publishing chief John Weber; my good friend Charles Defanti for his for invaluable editorial counsel and support; poet and esteemed copyeditor David Stanford Burr; Ashley Davis and her partner, Jonathan, for typographical and graphic support; my brilliant, multi-talented friend Craig Rubano, for sharing his literary sensibility, Apple eye, and musical ear; and, finally, for characterizing my work as *epiphanic*, my ten year-old grandson, Jack.

He had seventy-two hours to change the president and the course of history —or be killed trying.

Insurgents within the White House retain a uniquely gifted psychologist to help United States president George W. Bush address a clandestine addiction to alcohol and reverse the course of the Iraq War. The assignment meets with astonishing success—until foul forces come into play.

"A winner—a 'what if' novel wrapped in layers of reality that offers an unnerving 'case study' of alcoholism in the White House. We enter a series of psychological and forensic intelligence forays engendered by the U.S. secret service along with a certain Dr. Mark Alter, leadership psychologist and wizard at 'coaching' CEO's into restoring their acumen and performance. In this case, however, the patient is none other than President George W. Bush."

—Christian Science Monitor

"A literary and political masterpiece." **—Malachy McCourt,**
Green Party candidate for governor of New York State

"Unique, highly recommended, and sure to please . . .
Told from the perspective of the president's psychologist, this is a story with a unique twist and perspective."

—Midwest Reviews

Welcome Rain Publishers, LLC

New York

J ust as his big-time dreams seem about to come true, Chandler Haste glances into the rear view mirror of the limousine bearing him across Manhattan's Triboro Bridge, and catches the reflection of a scorching affair from his past overleaping oceans to engulf him.

"**Dazzling** . . . a delicious literary bonbon . . . **ranks among the finest novels ever.**" —*New York Observer* "**Inspired .** . . philosophically savvy, **hilarious,** whimsical." — *Kirkus Reviews* "**Stunning** . . . an ardent . . . an affecting . . . assured exploration of moral quandaries."—*Publishers Weekly* "**Poetic gold!** The finest contemporary showcasing of the sonnet form."—Charles Defanti, professor of literature, and author of *The Wages of Expectation; the Biography of Edward Dahlberg.* "**Shattering** . . . Those who find their wisdom in **wild and witty** packaging will love *Chancey* . . . **deeply moving.**"—Bernard Berkowitz, Ph.D. author of *How to Be Your Own Best Friend* "**Magnificent** . . . **racy and contentious** . . . literary and erudite . . . **profound and moving.** Captures the inner conflicts of conscience and provides **authentic insights** into the struggles of upward strivers."— Harry Levinson, clinical psychologist, Harvard Medical School

Welcome Rain Publishers, LLC

 New York

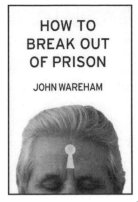

HOW TO
BREAK OUT
OF PRISON

JOHN WAREHAM

Unlock the Mind and go free now

True liberty begins with John Wareham's key insight: "All prisons are mental prisons; they lock from the inside and you own the key, so only you can let yourself out."

"Invigorating—bold ideas and an almost cocky tone combine with charm and edgy intricate logic to create a book that will result in a fresh and energized perspective." **—Library Journal**

"Powerful . . . Wareham's unusual premise, readable real-life examples, and self-assessment personality quizzes will appeal to those seeking to change their lives." **—Publishers Weekly**

"Astonishing . . . showcases Wareham's gift for unlocking the mind and showing us how to live the life of our deepest dreams." **—Kevin Roberts, Chief Executive, Saatchi & Saatchi.**

"A moving, life-altering work, uniquely honed in the disparate corridors of money and power, hope, and despair." **—Howard Frank, Ph.D., Dean, Maryland Business School**

Welcome Rain Publishers, LLC

 New York

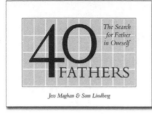

Who Would I Be If My Father Had Been Someone Else?

This startling and beautiful book is a valiant attempt to answer this universal and searching question by mining the recollections of forty sons and daughters from every imaginable background. The forty portraits are limited to two 350-word paragraphs of each subject's own words. The recollection of each father, accompanied by an archival photograph, is paired with a moving evaluation of the son's or daughter's heritage, and illustrated by a contemporary portrait. The result of a lifetime's research, this book is unlike any other study published.

Jess Maghan recently retired as professor of criminal justice at the University of Illinois at Chicago. *Sam Lindberg* has had a long career as a professional photographer, having collaborated with Irving Penn and other distinguished artists.

"Pay attention, literary world: The memoir has been reinvented."
— **Lary Bloom,** author, *The Writer Within,*
Letters From Nuremberg

"This remarkable book will awaken memories and open doors of understanding. You will smile, you will cry and you will thank the authors for this powerful testimony to the importance of fatherhood. This is a work that will transform your life."   — **Matthew Lippman,**
Ph.D., J.D., LL.M,
University of Illinois
professor of political science.

Corner of a Foreign Field:
Illustrated Poetry of the First World War

Crisp, contemporary *Daily Mail* photographs of World War I battle-fields, battles, and heartbreaking homefront scenes, complement poems written during the war, many by eminent writers, but most, by brilliant unsung poets.

The Artist's Wife by Max Phillips

"Alma Mahler Gropius, the 'wild brat' of fin-de-siecle Vienna, is the graceless subject of Phillips's (Snakebite Sonnet) bitingly sarcastic historical novel. Alma's forthright narration succeeds in conveying the personality of a complex, indomitable woman who behaved 'more like a man than a woman,' fascinated Vienna's art world and, later, Hollywood's expatriate colony, and who lived life exactly as she wished, bravely and without hypocrisy."—*Publishers Weekly*

That Summer's Trance by J. R. Salamanca

"Relentless, dignified, haunted by the future as well as the past, Salamanca's new work deserves a broad welcome and serious attention."—*Publishers Weekly*

Appointment with Il Duce by Hozy Rossi

"A stunning literary debut imbued with passion, honor, and tragedy."—*Booklist*

The Exquisite Life of Oscar Wilde by Stephen Calloway and David Colvin.

A sumptously illustrated coffee-table tome that tells the story and captures the spirit and times of the central figure of the fin de siècle, the literary genius who rose and fell—then rose again

Heart's Journey in Winter by James Buchan

The final battle of the Cold War is about to begin—a secret battle for the divided heart of Germany.

Welcome Rain Publishers, LLC

New York